Calculus for Middle Schoolers

Sunhut Publishing

Seattle, Washington

Library of Congress Control Number: 2020911467

ISBN: 978-0-578-71275-8

TABLE OF CONTENTS

PRECALCULUS

CALCULUS

WHY LEARN CALCULUS NOW?

Calculus is a whole new set of rules for students to learn, usually all at once at the end of high school. It can feel a bit overwhelming because there is a lot to learn in a short amount of time. The point of this book is to familiarize you with some important symbols and tools of precalculus that you will need to be successful in calculus, and then to teach you the fundamental calculus concepts. Learning these things early will help you feel comfortable with the basics and confident from the start. Hopefully, with a good foundation, you can appreciate the usefulness of calculus and perhaps even enjoy it!

Calculus is amazingly useful and can enable you to solve some pretty interesting problems, like:

- how to figure out the volumes of weirdly shaped containers,
- how to calculate the velocity of a car at each instant during acceleration,
- how to optimize the size of a container to fit the most product with the least amount of packaging,
- how to price merchandise in changing circumstances to maximize profit, and
- how to predict the path of a rocket at any given moment after launch.

Economists, physicists, biologists, engineers, chemists, statisticians and medical researchers all use calculus. So it is worth knowing!

PRECALCULUS

e

One term that you will see a lot in calculus is e. Many students freak out when they see e in a problem, but seriously, how could you not like a face like this?

e is just a constant like ***π*** that stands for an actual number. Both ***π*** and ***e*** are irrational numbers, meaning they go on and on forever without repeating. Rounded to the hundred thousandths place, the value of ***π*** equals 3.14159; also rounded to the hundred thousandths place, the value of ***e*** equals 2.71828.

e might look like a variable, but it never is. Its exact value is always the same. When you see ***e*** in a problem, just know that it stands for an actual number.

So, why is ***e*** so special? There are a few reasons (a couple of which are shown in the last chapter of this book).

One example that shows how ***e*** is special has to do with compound interest. Compound interest is when a bank gives you a portion of the interest you have earned for the year early, then lets you earn interest on that interest (as well as on the rest of your money) for the rest of the year.

The bank can do this once per year (interest would be compounded one time), each month (interest would be compounded 12 times), daily (interest would be compounded 365 times), or continuously (interest would be compounded an infinite number of times).

It turns out that if you invest $1 at 100% interest for one year, and the interest gets compounded continuously, the total amount you would have at the end of the year would "approach" $2.71828, which is the value of ***e***! No matter how many times the bank compounds that 100% interest on that one dollar, the total amount of your money will never go higher than ***e***.

Note: this idea of "approaching" a number is discussed in the chapter called "Lim" which stands for "limits."

I'm famous
for a r**e**ason!

PROBLEMS

1) $1 + e =$

Answer: Just substitute 2.718 for e. (I rounded to the thousandths place here)

$1 + e = \quad 1 + 2.718 = \quad$ **3.718**

2) $\frac{1}{e} =$

Answer: Again, substitute 2.718 for e.

$\frac{1}{e} = \quad \frac{1}{2.718} = \quad$ **0.368**

3) $e^0 =$

Answer: Anything with an exponent of zero equals 1.

$e^0 = \quad$ **1**

log

Another very useful concept to get comfortable with are logarithms, also called logs. Logs are just a handy tool that lets you solve for a variable when the variable is found in the exponent, like this: $10^x = 100$.

One way to understand logs is that they are just another way of writing an Exponential Equation. Every Exponential Equation can be rewritten as a Log Equation, and vice versa, just by rearranging the numbers.

Exponential Equation: $10^x = 100$ (read "ten to the x power equals 100")

Log Equation: $\log_{10} 100 = x$ (read "log base ten of 100 equals x")

In both of the above equations:

- The Base is 10
- The Exponent is x
- The Result is 100

The trick is knowing where to put the numbers. Here is where the numbers go in each type of equation:

For Exponential Equations: $\text{Base}^{\text{Exponent}} = \text{Result}$

For Log Equations: $\log_{\text{Base}} \text{Result} = \text{Exponent}$

Sometimes, if the problem is simple enough, you can solve a Log Equation just by re-writing it into an Exponential Equation. Let's try rewriting this Log Problem:

$\log_{10} 100 = x$

Use the Exponential Equation format $\text{Base}^{\text{Exponent}} = \text{Result}$ to rewrite into:

$10^x = 100$

Now, you can figure this out in your head: How many 10s do you multiply together in order to get an answer of 100? You multiply 2 of them together (10 * 10), so the exponent x must equal 2. The answer is

$x = 2$

In this problem, we didn't need to work with logs at all because we could figure out the answer just by rearranging into an Exponential Equation.

However, a lot of log problems cannot be solved this way. Here is an example:

$\log_{10} 27 = x$

Try rewriting it into the Exponential Equation format:

$\text{Base}^{\text{Exponent}} = \text{Result}$

$10^{x} = 27$

You can't do this one in your head! Putting this into Exponential Equation format did not help you because the Exponent x is not going to be a whole number.

Logs were invented to help with just this kind of problem. Using the Log Equation and a calculator, you can solve these problems easily!

Calculators have special buttons for calculating logs:

- If the base is 10 – use the button labeled "log"
- If the base is ***e*** – use the button labeled "ln" (we'll talk about this in the next chapter)

You can use these buttons on a calculator to answer log equations that have either of these two bases (and ONLY these two bases). So, for example, you can now solve

$\log_{10} 27 = x$

with the log button on a calculator because the Base is 10. Depending on your calculator, you put in the 27 first, then press the log button, OR you press the log button first, then 27, then press enter (or the equal sign "="). The calculator should tell you the answer is 1.431.

What you just found is the Exponent x. Now you know that you have to raise 10 to the power of 1.431 to get 27. That would look like this:

$10^{1.431} = 27$

(Note: 1.431 is rounded, so $10^{1.431}$ would equal 26.977, not exactly 27).

There is no way you could have figured that out in your head! However, by using the Log Equation format and the log button on your calculator, you can get the answer very easily.

Working with logs with a base of 10 is so common that people don't even bother writing "10" if that is the base in the Log Equation. So, in a Log Equation, if there is no base written, it has an assumed base of 10. Using this rule, these two Log Equations are exactly the same:

$\log 10 = x$ ⟵ is the same as ⟶ $\log_{10} 10 = x$

(By the way, the answer to this Log Equation is 1. You can either use the log button on your calculator to find the answer or rewrite as the Exponential Equation $10^x = 10$ and see that the Exponent x must be 1).

PROBLEMS

1) Rewrite the Exponential Equation 10^x = 16 into a Log Equation, then solve for x.

   Answer: Compare your given equation to the Exponential Equation format:

   $\text{Base}^{\text{Exponent}}$ = Result
   10^x = 16

   From this, you can see that the Base is 10, the Exponent is x, and the Result is 16. Rearrange these terms into the Log Equation format:

   $\log_{\text{Base}} \text{Result}$ = Exponent
   $\log_{10} 16 = x$

   So, that is the first part of your answer: the Log Equation is

   $\mathbf{\log_{10} 16 = x}$

Remember that you don't need to put 10 as the Base, because it is understood. So, you could also just write your answer like this:

$$\log 16 = x$$

The second part of the question is to solve for x. Because the Base is 10 in this problem, you can use the log button on your calculator. Just put in the 16 first, then press the log button (or, depending on your calculator, press the log button, then 16, then press enter or =), and you will get:

$$x = 1.204$$

This means that you have to raise 10 to the power of 1.204 to get 16. That would look like this: $10^{1.204}$ = 16. There is no way you could have figured that out without using logs!

(Note: 1.204 is rounded, so $10^{1.204}$ would equal 15.996, not exactly 16).

2) Rewrite $\log_{10} 10{,}000 = x$ into an Exponential Equation, then solve for x.

Answer: Compare your given equation to the Log Equation format:

$\log_{\text{Base}} \text{Result} = \text{Exponent}$
$\log_{10} 10{,}000 = x$

From this, you can see that the Base is 10, the Result is 10,000, and the Exponent is x. Rearrange these terms into the Exponential format:

$\text{Base}^{\text{Exponent}} = \text{Result}$
$10^x = 10{,}000$

So, that is the first part of your answer: the Exponential Equation is

$$10^x = 10{,}000$$

Looking at the Exponential Equation, you can figure out in your head (just count the zeroes) that you have to multiply 4 number 10s together (10 * 10 * 10 * 10) to get 10,000, so the Exponent x equals 4.

$$x = 4$$

Alternatively, since the Base in the Log Equation is 10, you can use the $\log$ button on a calculator to solve $\log_{10} 10{,}000 = x$. Just put in the 10,000, then press the $\log$ button (or, depending on your calculator, press the $\log$ button, then 10,000, then press enter or =), and you will get the same answer: 4.

3) $\log_5 25 = x$

Answer: Because the base is not 10 or $\boldsymbol{e}$, we can't use the log or ln buttons on the calculator. Instead, let's rewrite. Compare your given equation to the Log Equation format:

$\log_{\text{Base}} \text{Result} = \text{Exponent}$
$\log_5 25 = x$

From this, you can see that the Base is 5, the Result is 25, and the Exponent is x. Rearrange these terms into the Exponential format:

$\text{Base}^{\text{Exponent}} = \text{Result}$
$5^x = 25$

You can figure out in your head that you have to multiply 2 number 5s together (5 * 5) to get 25, therefore the exponent is 2. The answer is

$x = 2$

Note: There *is* a way to solve Log Equations like this (where the base is not 10 or $\boldsymbol{e}$) with the buttons on a calculator. You just need to use something called the

"Change of Base Formula," which we won't cover in this book.

4) $\log 25 = x$

Answer: Remember, if there is no base included in the Log Equation, assume the Base is 10. Use a calculator to solve: just put in 25, then press the log button (or, depending on your calculator, press the log button, then 25, then press enter or =), and you will get

$x = 1.398$

Just to see what this means, let's rewrite. Compare your given equation to the Log Equation format (remember that we already said the Base must be 10):

$\log_{\text{Base}} \text{Result} = \text{Exponent}$
$\log_{10} 25 = x$

From this, you can see that the Base is 10, the Result is 25, and the Exponent is x. Rearrange these terms into the Exponential format:

$\text{Base}^{\text{Exponent}} = \text{Result}$
$10^{x} = 25$

Now fill in what we found: that x = 1.398:

$10^{1.398}$ = 25

Again, think about how difficult it would have been to find that Exponent answer without using logs!

(Note: 1.398 is rounded, so $10^{1.398}$ would equal 25.003, not exactly 25).

ln

A special case in logs is when the log has a base of e. Because e is such a terrific and useful number, a log with a base of e has a special name: "natural log," written "ln."

When you say "ln" out loud, you just say the letters one after another: "L" "N." So, for example, ln 20 is read "L," "N," "twenty."

When you see ln, you can always just replace it with $\log_e$ because they mean the same thing!

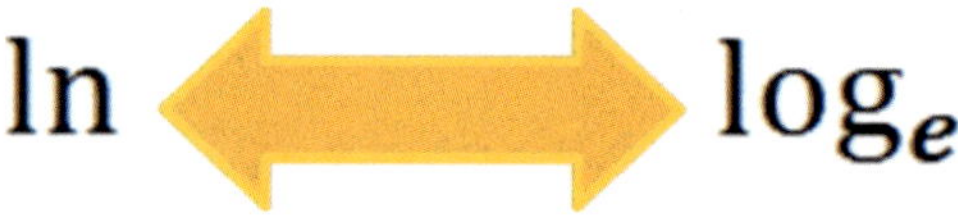

For example, $\ln 100 = x$ is the same as $\log_e 100 = x$.

As mentioned before, there is a special button labeled "ln" on the calculator. For the answer to the problem $\ln 100 = x$ (shown above), you would put in 100 then press the ln button (or, depending on your calculator, you would press the ln button, then 100, then press enter or =). The answer is

$x = 4.605$

To see what this means, let's rewrite. Compare the equation we started with to the Log Equation format:

$\log_{\text{Base}} \text{Result} = \text{Exponent}$
$\log_{e} 100 = x$

From this, you can see that the Base is e, the Result is 100, and the Exponent is x. Rearrange these terms into the Exponential format:

$\text{Base}^{\text{Exponent}} = \text{Result}$
$e^{x} = 100$

Now fill in what we found with the calculator: that $x = 4.605$:

$e^{4.605} = 100$

That means you would have to raise e to the power of 4.605 in order to get 100. (Note: 4.605 is rounded, so $e^{4.605}$ would equal 99.983, not exactly 100).

Hello, my name is Ellen. My loyal pet named ***e*** goes everywhere with me. I would be lost without him!
e
l n

PROBLEMS

1) Rewrite the Exponential Equation $\boldsymbol{e}^x = 5$ into a Log Equation.

Answer: Compare your given equation to the Exponential Equation format:

$\text{Base}^{\text{Exponent}} = \text{Result}$
$\boldsymbol{e}^x = 5$

From this, you can see that the Base is $\boldsymbol{e}$, the Exponent is x, and the Result is 5. Rearrange these terms into the Log Equation format:

$\log_{\text{Base}} \text{Result} = \text{Exponent}$
$\log_e 5 = x$

Since any time we see $\log_{\mathrm{e}}$ we can just replace it with ln, the rewritten Log Equation is

$\ln 5 = x$

2) Solve for x in the Log Equation $\ln 5 = x$

Answer: Use a calculator because usually you can't do $\ln$ problems in your head. Either put in 5, then press the $\ln$ button (or, depending on your calculator, press the $\ln$ button, then 5, then press enter or =) to get the answer:

$$x = 1.609$$

To see what this means, go back to the original Exponential Equation from problem 1:

$\boldsymbol{e}^x = 5$

Now fill in what we found with the calculator, that $x = 1.609$:

$\boldsymbol{e}^{1.609} = 5$

This means that you would have to raise $\boldsymbol{e}$ to the power of 1.609 (roughly, because it is rounded) to get the Result 5.

3) $\ln 1 = x$

Answer: To solve using a calculator, put in 1, then press the ln button (or, depending on your calculator, press the ln button, then 1, then press enter or =) to get the answer:

$x = 0$

However, this is an ln problem you can actually do in your head, so let's do it that way, too.

To solve without a calculator, start with the given problem:

$\ln 1 = x$, then replace ln with $\log_e$:

$\log_e 1 = x$, then compare to the Log Equation format:

$\log_{\text{Base}} \text{Result} = \text{Exponent}$

From this, you can see that the Base is e, the Result is 1, and the Exponent is x. Rearrange these terms into the Exponential format:

$\text{Base}^{\text{Exponent}} = \text{Result}$
$e^x = 1$

Remember that an exponent of zero always gives the Result of 1. Since the Result here is 1, you know that the Exponent (x) must be zero (confirming the answer that we found using the calculator).

trig

Trigonometry comes up a lot in calculus problems, so having a good understanding of trig is extremely helpful.

The basics of trig start with a right triangle (a right triangle is a triangle that has a 90° angle in it). In a right triangle, if you know the measure of one angle (besides the 90° angle), trig will tell you what the ratios of the side lengths are to each other.

Look at the two right triangles in the picture below. They each have a given angle measure of 30°. I labeled the side opposite the 30° angle "***opposite***," the side across from the 90° angle "***hypotenuse***," and the side next to the 30° angle (but not the hypotenuse) "***adjacent***" because adjacent means "next to." The numbers shown are the lengths of the sides.

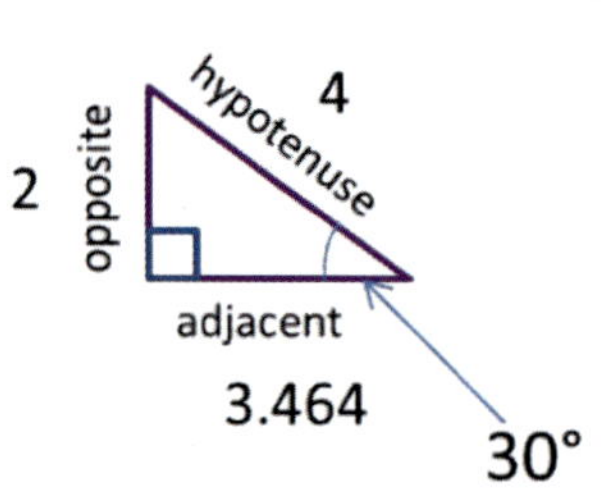

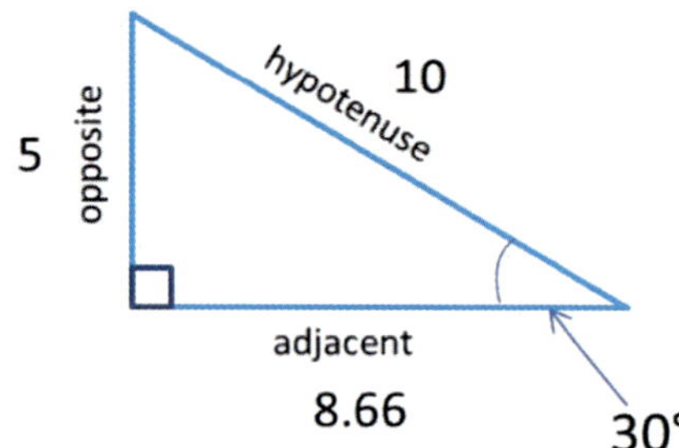

You can see that the side lengths are different between the two triangles. However, as shown below, the two triangles have the same side length ***ratios***. That is because the angle, in this case 30°, dictates what these side length ratios are.

Let's look at the ratio of ***opposite*** to ***hypotenuse.***

In the small triangle, the ratio is

$$\frac{opposite}{hypotenuse} = \frac{2}{4} = \frac{1}{2} = 0.5$$

In the big triangle, the ratio is

$$\frac{opposite}{hypotenuse} = \frac{5}{10} = \frac{1}{2} = 0.5$$

The ratio of the opposite side to the hypotenuse is always 0.5 in any right triangle when you are dealing with a 30° angle.

Now let's look at the ratio of ***adjacent*** to ***hypotenuse*.**

In the small triangle, the ratio is

$$\frac{adjacent}{hypotenuse} = \frac{3.464}{4} = 0.866$$

In the big triangle, the ratio is

$$\frac{adjacent}{hypotenuse} = \frac{8.66}{10} = 0.866$$

Again, the ratio is the same! The ratio of the adjacent side to the hypotenuse is always 0.866 in any right triangle when you are dealing with a 30° angle.

Finally, let's look at the ratio of ***opposite*** to ***adjacent***.

In the small triangle, the ratio is

$$\frac{opposite}{adjacent} = \frac{2}{3.464} = 0.577$$

In the big triangle, the ratio is

$$\frac{opposite}{adjacent} = \frac{5}{8.66} = 0.577$$

Not surprisingly, the ratio is the same. The ratio of the opposite side to the adjacent side is always 0.577 in any right triangle when you are dealing with a 30° angle.

What you just learned are the three basic trig functions: sine, cosine, and tangent! The trig functions are just the highlighted ratios we just discussed.

Here are the definitions of the three basic trig ratios, as well as the shorthand that uses the symbol θ (called "theta") to represent any angle:

The sine of an angle equals $\frac{opposite}{hypotenuse}$ ➡ $\sin\theta = \frac{opp}{hyp}$

The cosine of an angle equals $\frac{adjacent}{hypotenuse}$ ➡ $\cos\theta = \frac{adj}{hyp}$

The tangent of an angle equals $\frac{opposite}{adjacent}$ ➡ $\tan\theta = \frac{opp}{adj}$

Every angle has its own sine, cosine, and tangent ratios. So, if you were dealing with a 31° angle, for example, the answers would be different than the ones we found here for a 30° angle. In other words, a right triangle with a 31° angle would have sides in slightly different ratios to each other than a right triangle with a 30° angle.

Trig gives you the ratios of all the sides to each other, based on what angle you have in your right triangle. So, if you know one angle (other than the 90° angle) and one side length, you can find the lengths of the other sides using these ratios. This makes trig extremely useful for finding unknown lengths of things that are difficult to measure, like the height of a really tall tree or the width of a raging river that you can't cross.

For example, suppose you are trying to figure out how much a tree grows each year. Imagine each year having to climb that tree with a measuring tape!

You can use trig instead. All you need is 1) the length of a line on the ground starting at the bottom of the tree and 2) the measure of the angle between that line and a line that would reach from the end of it to the top of the tree (there are instruments that make measuring this angle easy).

The following picture shows the right triangle that is formed as well as example measurements, which are shown in green. You can use a trig ratio to calculate the missing side (height of the tree).

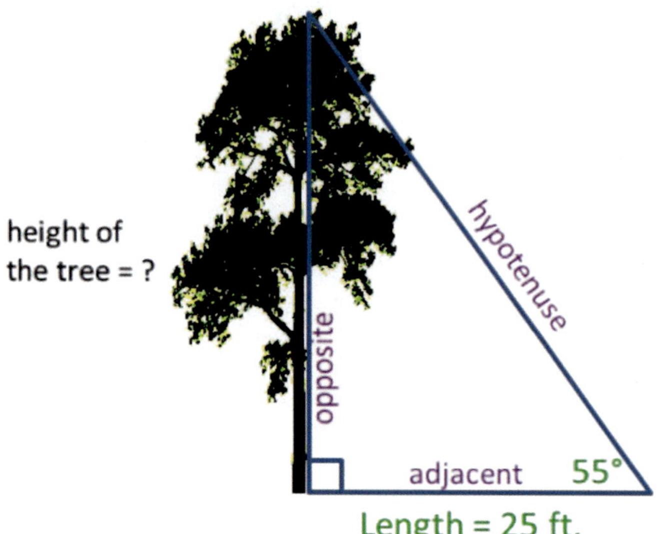

In this problem, the side we know is the adjacent side and the side we want to find out is the opposite side. So, use the trig ratio that deals with those two sides, which is tangent.

tan $\theta = \frac{opp}{adj}$

Next, fill in the information we know:

tan55° = $\frac{opp}{25}$

Now, using algebra, multiply both sides of the equation by 25:

tan55° * 25 = opp

Use your calculator to find the answer. Enter 55, then the "tan" button (or, depending on your calculator, press the "tan" button, then 55, then press enter or =), and then multiply by 25. You will get the answer 35.7 ft. You just found the height of the tree without leaving the ground!

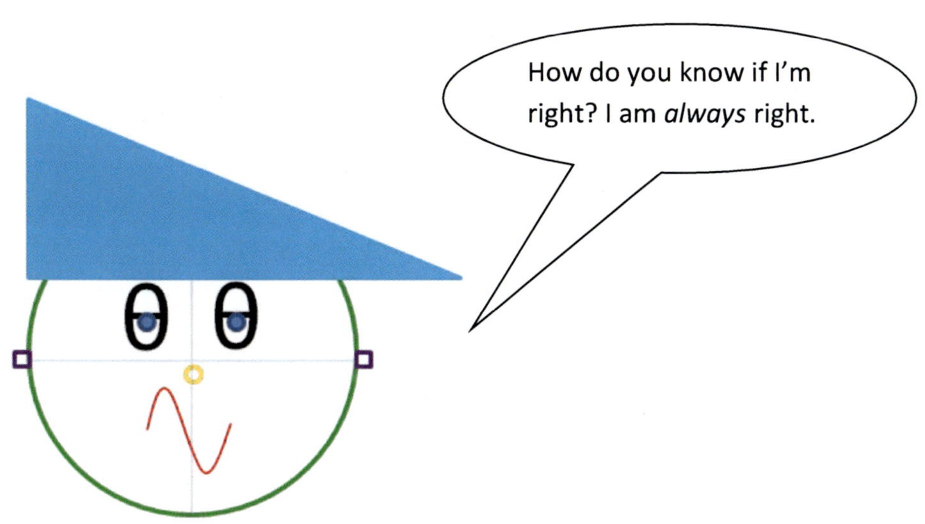

So far, we have been talking about trigonometry in right triangles. Now, we will look at how these same trig ratios can be found in a circle.

A very useful tool in trig is the unit circle. A unit circle is a circle that is centered at the point (0, 0) and has a radius of one. Here is a picture:

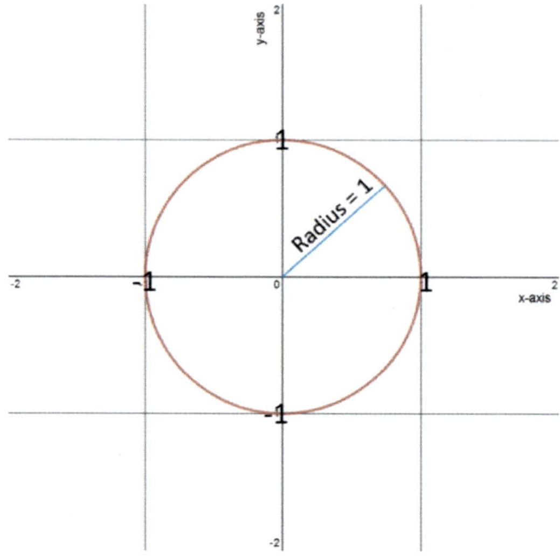

The reason why this is such a useful tool is that you can pick off the cosine and sine of any angle just by looking at the x and y coordinates of the points along the circle.

(cosine, sine)

↓ ↓

(x, y)

In the picture below, the radius makes a 30° angle with the x-axis. The x and y coordinates of the point where that radius touches the circle are the cosine and sine of that 30° angle (which we calculated in our earlier example).

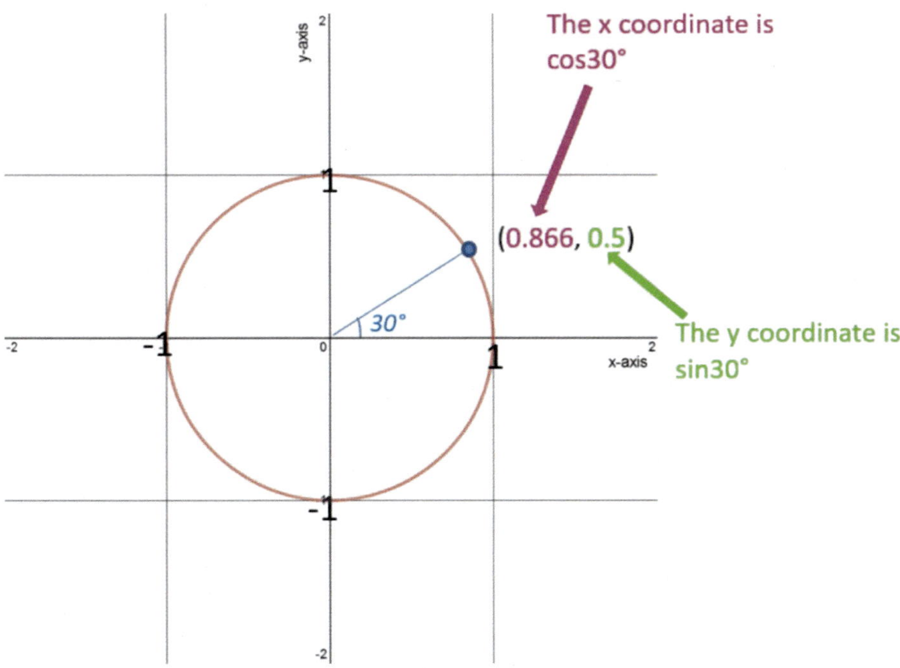

You can prove why this is the case. As shown in the next picture, if you drop down a line from the point (0.866, 0.5) to the x-axis, you can make a right triangle. The height of the triangle is the y value of 0.5, the base is the x value of 0.866, and the radius is 1 (because this is a unit circle and all the radii are equal in a circle). As you can see from the calculations on the picture, cos30° and sin30° do, indeed, come out to 0.866 and 0.5.

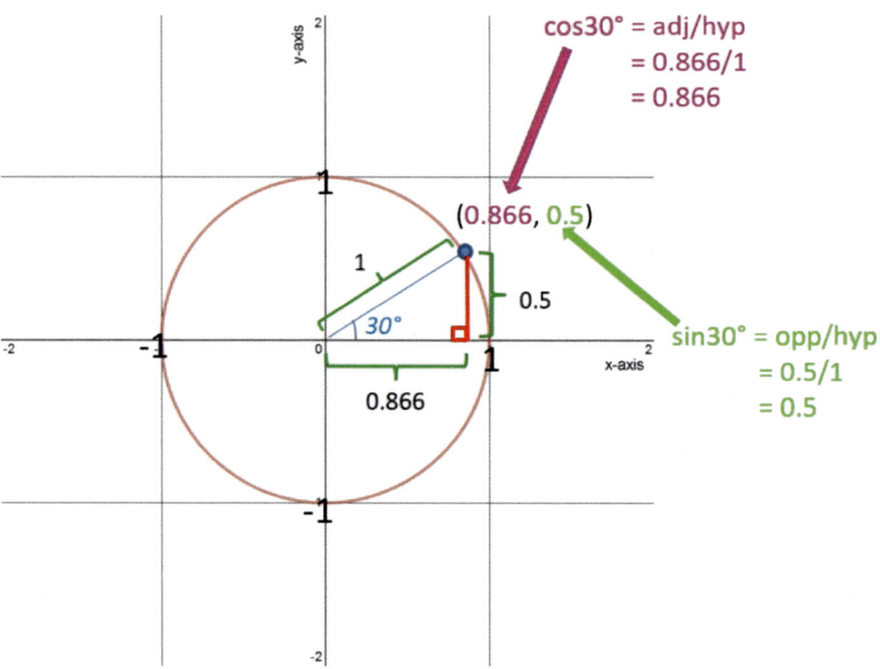

Just by looking at the x and y coordinates of the points along the unit circle, we can answer quite easily what the cosine and sine are of any angle. To show this, the following unit circle shows the cosine and sine of two important angles: 0° and 90°.

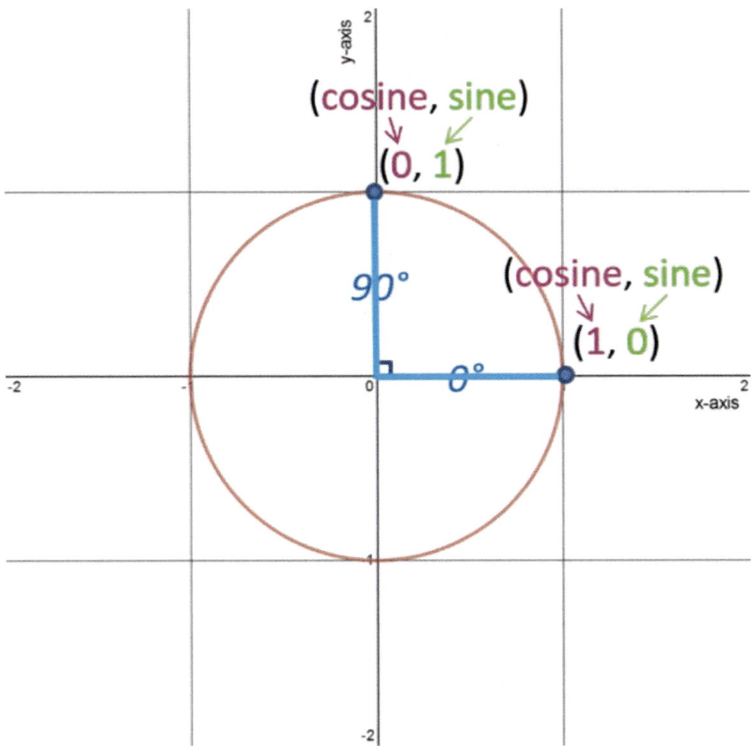

For the 0° angle above, the radius is 0° above the x-axis (which means it is resting on the x-axis), and the point where that radius touches the circle is the point (1, 0). Therefore, the cosine of 0° is 1 (the x-coordinate) and the sine of 0° is 0 (the y-coordinate).

Similarly, for the 90° angle above, the radius makes a 90° angle with the x-axis. The point where that radius touches the circle is the point (0, 1). Therefore, the cosine of 90° is 0 (the x-coordinate) and the sine of 90° is 1 (the y-coordinate).

It is handy to memorize the cosines and sines of important angles, since some particular angles come up a lot in problems.

The next graphs show the cosines and sines for these important angles: 30°, 45°, and 60°.

I have written them in fraction form (instead of with decimals like in my prior examples) because fraction form is how they are usually written. (Note that the fraction $\frac{\sqrt{3}}{2}$ is the same as 0.866, the decimal in our examples).

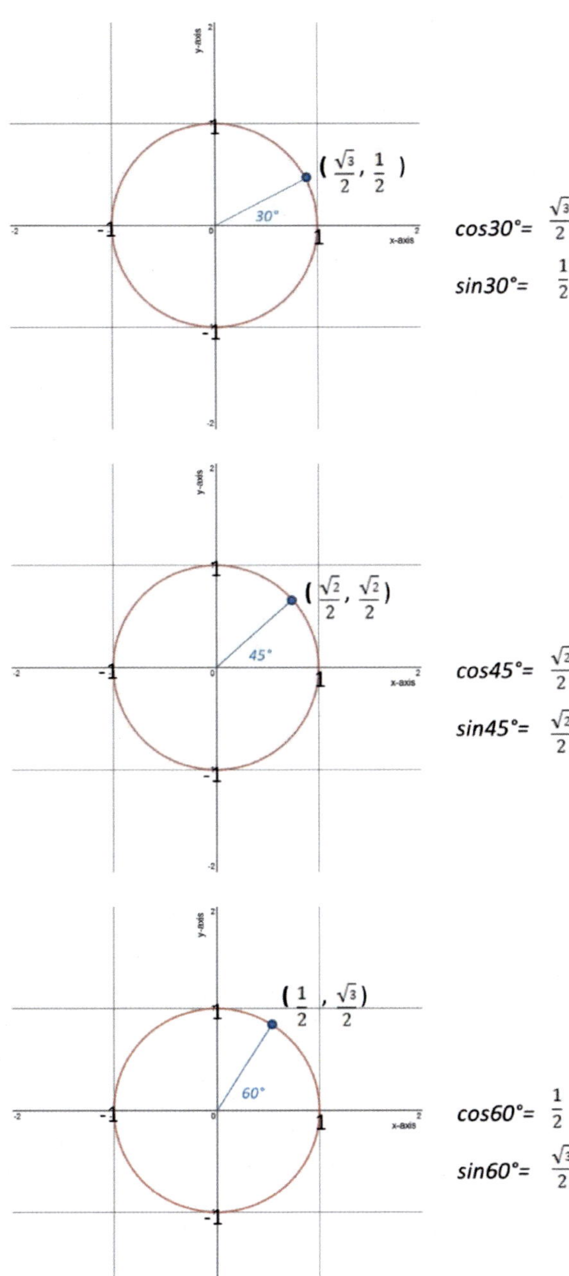
y-axis
x-axis
30°
$(\frac{\sqrt{3}}{2}, \frac{1}{2})$
$\cos 30° = \frac{\sqrt{3}}{2}$
$\sin 30° = \frac{1}{2}$
45°
$(\frac{\sqrt{2}}{2}, \frac{\sqrt{2}}{2})$
$\cos 45° = \frac{\sqrt{2}}{2}$
$\sin 45° = \frac{\sqrt{2}}{2}$
60°
$(\frac{1}{2}, \frac{\sqrt{3}}{2})$
$\cos 60° = \frac{1}{2}$
$\sin 60° = \frac{\sqrt{3}}{2}$

What about tangent? To figure out the tangent of an angle using the unit circle, you just need to know this very handy fact about tangent: tangent equals sine divided by cosine:

$$\tan\theta = \frac{\sin\theta}{\cos\theta}$$

So, for example, if you wanted to find the tangent of 60°, here is the calculation:

$$\tan 60° = \frac{\sin 60°}{\cos 60°} = \frac{\frac{\sqrt{3}}{2}}{\frac{1}{2}} = \frac{\sqrt{3}}{2} * \frac{2}{1} = \frac{\sqrt{3}}{1} = \sqrt{3}$$

(Notice how the problem required us to divide by $\frac{1}{2}$, so we multiplied by its reciprocal: $\frac{2}{1}$)

Sine, cosine and tangent each have their own distinctive curves. The graphs of sine, cosine and tangent are worth knowing because you see them often, both in textbooks and in the real world.

The graphs of these functions are repeating waves that can represent things like sound waves, light waves, radio waves, ocean waves, tides, and earthquakes.

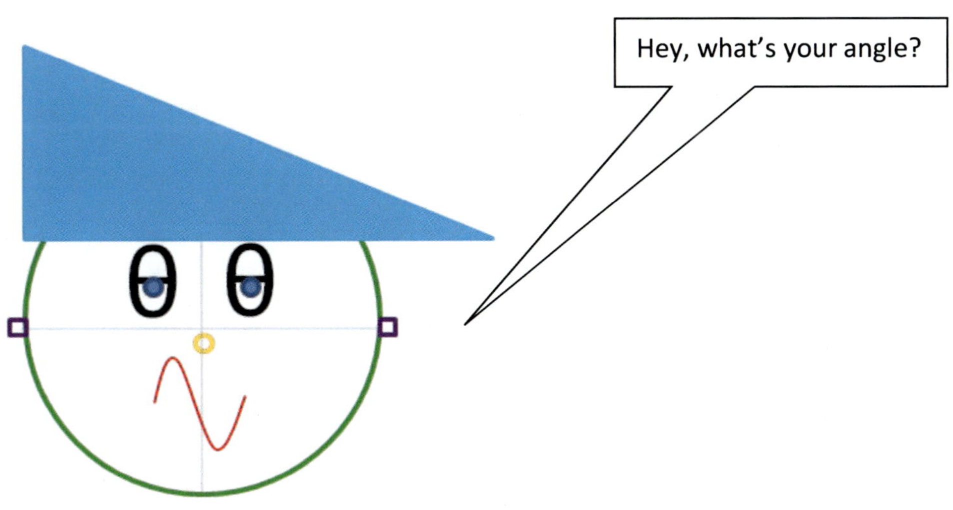

You can make the sine graph by "unwinding" the unit circle. The picture below shows the unit circle with the four points labeled where the radius forms a 0°, 90°, 180°, and 270° angle with the x-axis. Notice the sine value associated with each of these angles.

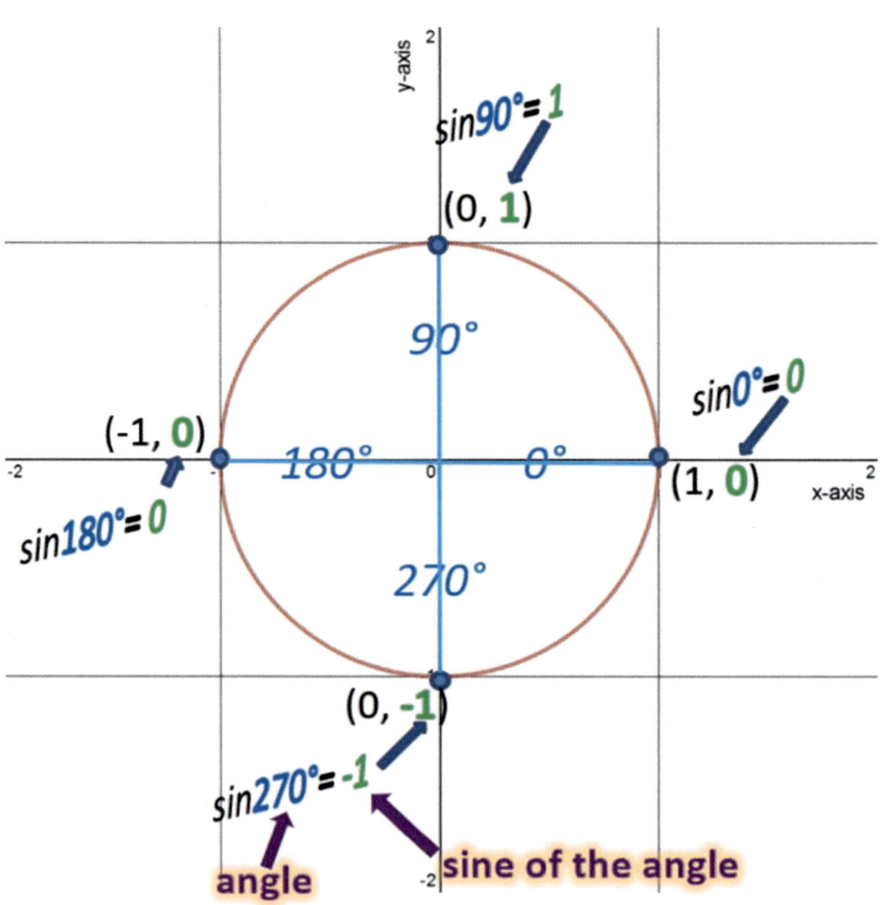

Here is the sine graph. On the x-axis are those same angle measures. On the y-axis are the sine values. So, the (x, y) points on the sine graph represent (angle, sine of the angle). Notice how these two pieces of information, angle and sine of the angle, appear in the unit circle and also in the sine graph. The sine graph is an up and down curve that goes on and on forever.

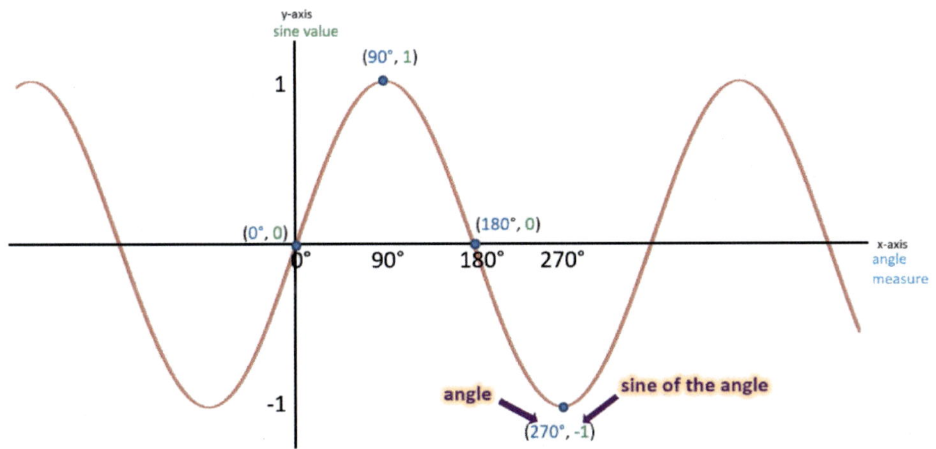

We can do the same "unwinding" to get the cosine graph. The picture below shows the same four points on the unit circle where the radius forms a 0°, 90°, 180°, and 270° angle with the x-axis. This time, we are interested in the cosine value at each angle measure.

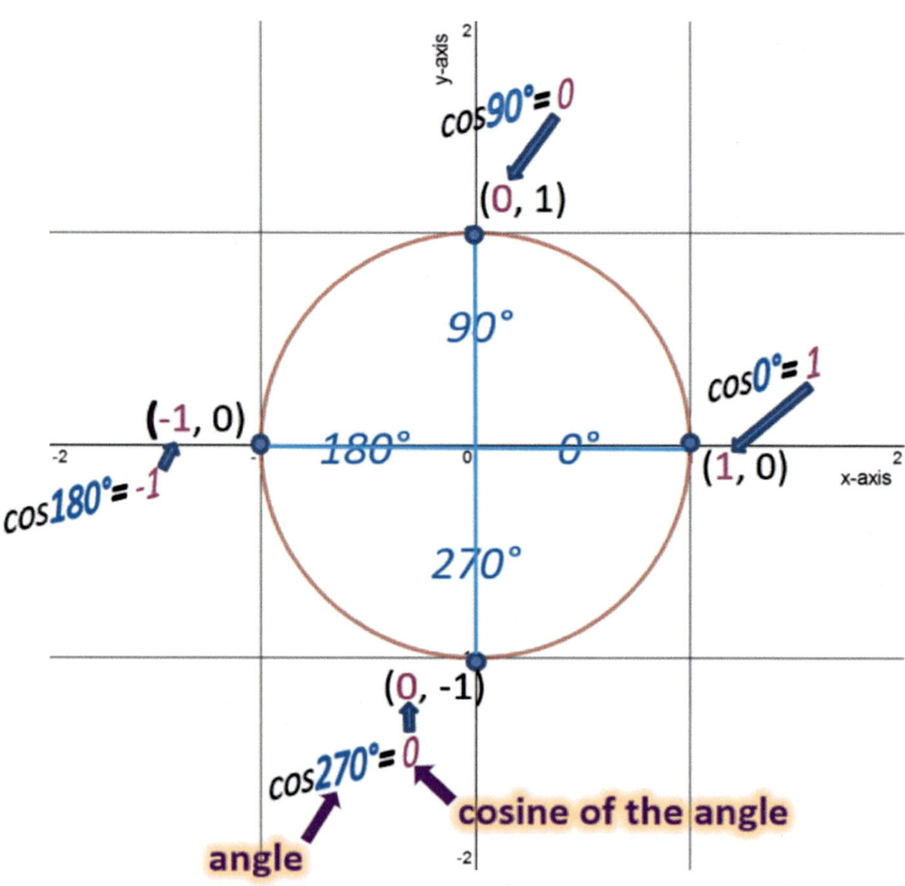

Here is the cosine graph. The x-axis shows the angle measures and the y-axis shows the cosine values. The (x, y) points on the cosine graph represent (angle, cosine of the angle). Notice how the two pieces of information, angle and cosine of the angle, appear in the unit circle and also in the cosine graph. Just like the sine graph, the cosine graph is an up and down curve that goes on and on forever.

Cosine Graph

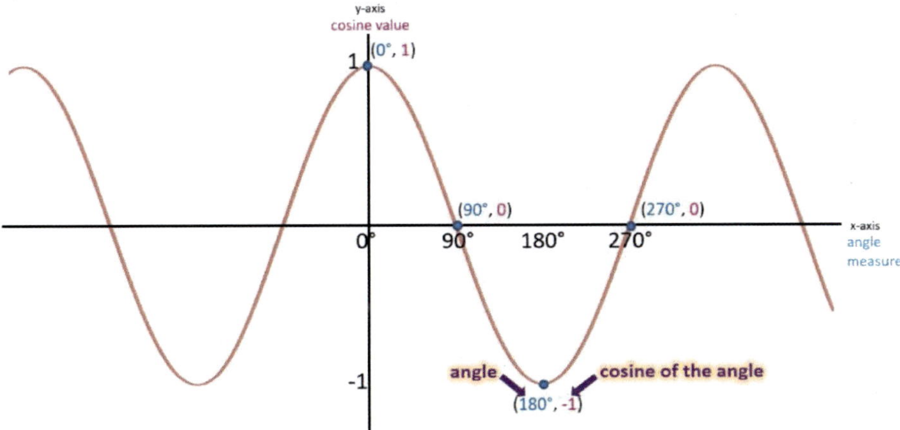

The cosine curve looks very similar to the sine curve. In fact, the only difference is where they start. The sine and cosine curves are the same curve, just 90° out of sync with each other.

The graph of the last trig ratio, tangent, looks quite a bit different. Earlier in the chapter, you learned

$$\tan\theta = \frac{\sin\theta}{\cos\theta}$$

Because you can't have zero in the denominator, there is no tangent value when cosine equals zero. Instead, at the points where cosine equals zero, the tangent graph will have ***asymptotes***, or lines that the curve will approach but never reach. These asymptotes, shown as dotted green lines on the next graph, occur everywhere cosine equals zero. Notice that since $\cos 90°$ and $\cos 270°$ equal zero, asymptotes occur at those angles.

When sine equals zero, the numerator of the tangent ratio is zero. So, tangent will equal zero when sine equals zero. Notice that since $\sin 0°$ and $\sin 180°$equal zero, tangent equals zero at those angles.

Tangent is a repeating curve, but it is interrupted again and again by the asymptotes. At each asymptote, the tangent value goes to infinity; the tangent curve approaches the asymptote but never reaches it.

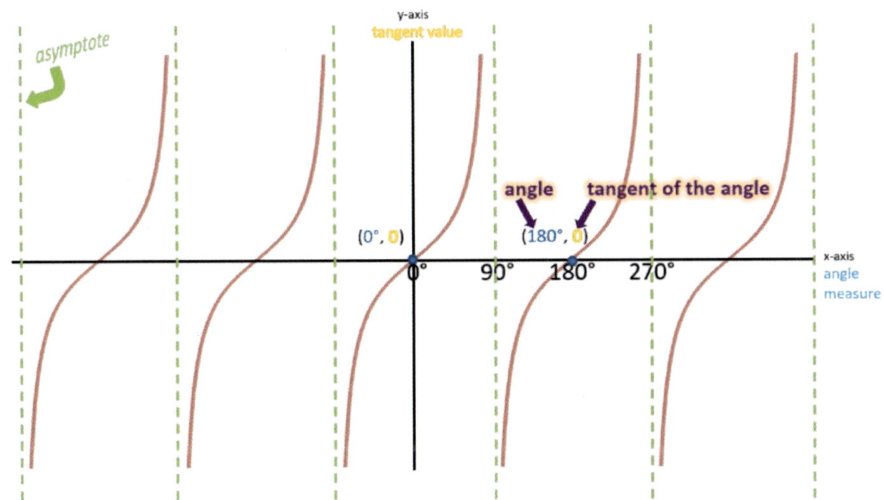

We have been talking so far about the three basic trig ratios. There are three more ratios that you need to know, but they are just the reciprocals of the ones you have already learned:

- cosecant (csc) is the reciprocal of sine
- secant (sec) is the reciprocal of cosine
- cotangent (cot) is the reciprocal of tangent

The reciprocal of a number is 1 over that number. The reciprocal is also the "flip" of a fraction. Here are the definitions of these new trig ratios:

cosecant: $\csc\theta = \dfrac{1}{\sin\theta} = \dfrac{hypotenuse}{opposite}$

secant: $\sec\theta = \dfrac{1}{\cos\theta} = \dfrac{hypotenuse}{adjacent}$

cotangent: $\cot\theta = \dfrac{1}{\tan\theta} = \dfrac{adjacent}{opposite}$

PROBLEMS

1) Find the sides of this right triangle if the hypotenuse measures 47 feet:

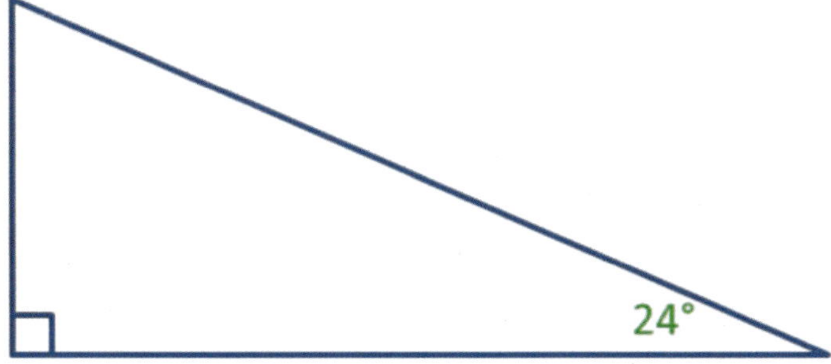

Answer: Here is the same triangle with the sides labeled:

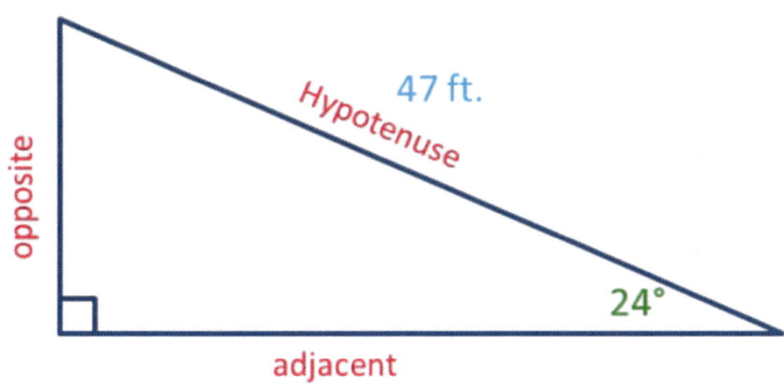

Let’s start by finding the opposite side. The side we know is the hypotenuse and the side we want to find is the opposite side. So, use the trig ratio that deals with those two sides, which is sine.

$\sin\theta = \frac{opp}{hyp}$

Next, fill in the information we know:

$\sin 24° = \frac{opp}{47}$

Now, using algebra, multiply both sides of the equation by 47:

$\sin 24° * 47 = opp$

Use your calculator to find the answer. Enter 24, then the “sin” button (or, depending on your calculator, press the “sin” button, then 24, then press enter or =), and then multiply by 47. You will get the answer 19.1.

The opposite side is 19.1 feet

Now, let's find the adjacent side. The side we know is the hypotenuse (keep using the given side as the "known" side), but now the side we want to find is the adjacent side. So, use the trig ratio that deals with those two sides, which is cosine.

$\cos\theta = \frac{adj}{hyp}$

Next, fill in the information we know:

$\cos 24° = \frac{adj}{47}$

Now, using algebra, multiply both sides of the equation by 47:

$\cos 24° * 47 = adj$

Use your calculator to find the answer. Enter 24, then the "cos" button (or, depending on your calculator, press the "cos" button, then 24, then press enter or =), and then multiply by 47. You will get the answer 42.9.

The adjacent side is 42.9 feet

2) Using a unit circle, find the sine, cosine and tangent of a 67° angle.

Answer: Below is a unit circle with a radius that forms a 67° angle with the x-axis. The point where this radius touches the circle is labeled.

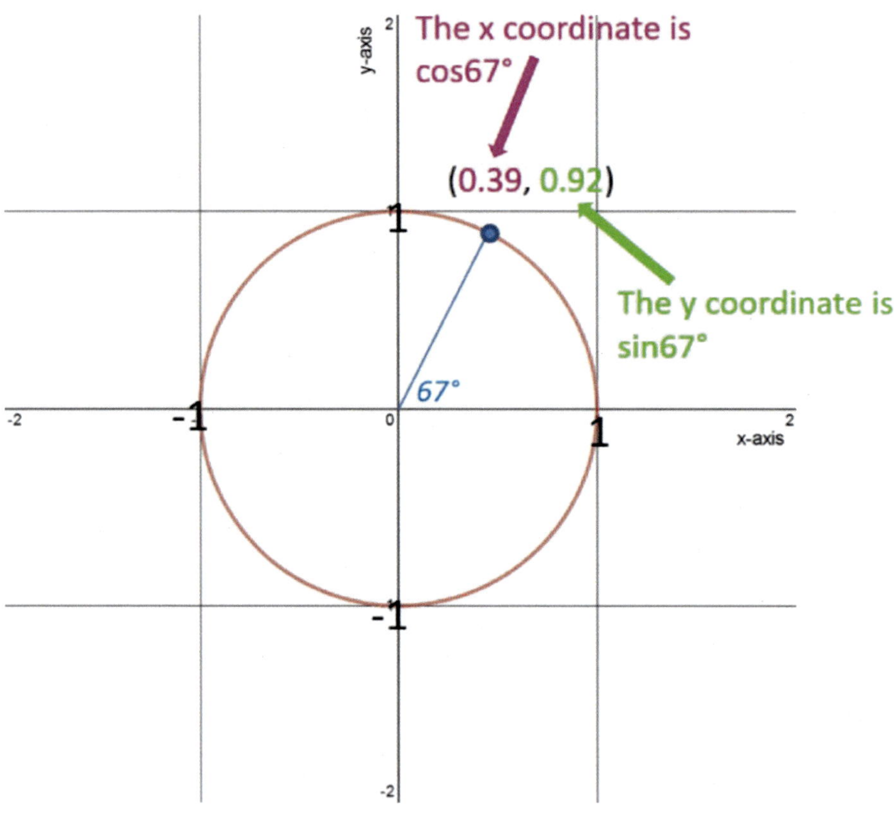

This graph gives the answers for the cosine and sine of 67° because they are just the x and y coordinates of the point. In order to find the tangent of 67°, use this definition of tangent:

$$\tan\theta = \frac{\sin\theta}{\cos\theta}$$

$$\tan\theta = \frac{0.92}{0.39} = 2.36$$

Here is the full answer:

sin67° = 0.92
cos67° = 0.39
tan67° = 2.36

Note: Use the "sin," "cos" and "tan" buttons on your calculator to check these answers. To confirm the answer for sine, for example, type in 67, then press the "sin" button (or, depending on your calculator, press the "sin" button, then 67, then press enter or =). You will get the same answers as we got above.

3) Find $\sec 67°$

Answer: By definition, the secant of an angle is the reciprocal of the cosine of an angle. Since we already found the cosine of 67° in problem 2, we just need to put 1 over that number:

$$\sec 67° = \frac{1}{\cos 67°} = \frac{1}{0.39} = 2.56$$

$\sec 67° = 2.56$

Σ

The symbol Σ, called sigma, tells you to take the sum of a list of numbers. It is written with notation on the bottom, on the top, and to the right, like this:

$$\sum_{i=0}^{4} \frac{i}{2} =$$

There are three parts of this summation problem to be aware of:

1) The $i = 0$ at the bottom of the Σ tells you that you start with the value of 0 for the variable i.

$$\sum_{i=0}^{4} \frac{i}{2} =$$

2) The 4 at the top of the Σ tells you that you end with the value of 4 for the variable i. (So, in this problem, you will use the numbers 0 through 4 for i).

$$\sum_{i=0}^{4} \frac{i}{2} =$$

3) To the right of the Σ is the operation you are plugging these numbers into.

$$\sum_{i=0}^{4} \frac{i}{2} =$$

To solve this problem, plug the numbers 0, 1, 2, 3 and 4 in for i, one at a time, into $\frac{i}{2}$. When you do this, you will get this list:

$$\frac{0}{2}, \frac{1}{2}, \frac{2}{2}, \frac{3}{2}, \frac{4}{2}$$

The next and final step is to add the numbers in your list together like this:

$$\frac{0}{2} + \frac{1}{2} + \frac{2}{2} + \frac{3}{2} + \frac{4}{2} = \frac{10}{2} = 5$$

So, the answer is

$$\sum_{i=0}^{4} \frac{i}{2} = 5$$

What you just found was the sum of a list of numbers, but there was no addition sign (+) in the original problem! By using Σ, problems can be written in a much shorter way. Instead of listing all those individual numbers to add up, like this:

$$\frac{0}{2} + \frac{1}{2} + \frac{2}{2} + \frac{3}{2} + \frac{4}{2} =$$

you can just write the problem like this:

$$\sum_{i=0}^{4} \frac{i}{2} =$$

Plus, some calculators have the ability to solve Σ problems just by entering a few numbers.

One interesting kind of Σ problem is when ∞ (infinity) is at the top of the symbol Σ. These problems are called infinite series problems because your list of numbers to add up goes on and on to infinity.

You might think that if you add up numbers forever, your answer would be ∞. However, this is where infinite series problems might surprise you. Sometimes the answer is ∞, but sometimes the series adds up to an actual number for an answer!

Here is an example of an infinite series that has an actual number for an answer:

$$\sum_{m=1}^{\infty} \frac{1}{2^m} =$$

Plug in the numbers 1, 2, 3, 4, and 5 for m into the operation to get the first few numbers in your list:

$$\frac{1}{2^1}, \frac{1}{2^2}, \frac{1}{2^3}, \frac{1}{2^4}, \frac{1}{2^5} \ldots\ldots\ldots\ldots\ldots$$

Then, add them up:

$$\frac{1}{2} + \frac{1}{4} + \frac{1}{8} + \frac{1}{16} + \frac{1}{32} + \ldots\ldots\ldots\ldots\ldots$$

If you add up these first few numbers, you get 0.96875. But, the fractions in this series keep getting smaller and smaller, so they are adding less and less to the total as the list goes on. If you keep adding up the next fractions in this series forever, you will actually get to the number one. The answer to this problem is

$$\sum_{m=1}^{\infty} \frac{1}{2^m} = 1$$

There are rules for finding the answers for these kinds of infinite series problems, which we won't go into in this book. For now, just know that sometimes the sum of an infinite series is infinity, but sometimes you end up at an actual number answer.

PROBLEMS

1) $\sum_{n=1}^{3} n^2 =$

Answer: In this problem, the variable is n. Start with a value for n of 1 and end with a value for n of 3, so the numbers you will use for n are 1, 2, and 3. Now, plug these numbers, one at a time, into the operation n^2. When you do this, you get this sequence:

$1^2, 2^2, 3^2$

Now add the numbers in your sequence together:

$1^2 + 2^2 + 3^2 = \quad 1 + 4 + 9 = \quad 14$

So, here is the answer:

$$\sum_{n=1}^{3} n^2 = 14$$

$$2)\ \sum_{k=3}^{6} k + 2 =$$

Answer: In this problem, the variable is k. Start with a value for k of 3 and end with a value for k of 6, so the numbers you will use for k are 3, 4, 5, and 6. Now, plug these numbers, one at a time, into the operation $k + 2$, and add them all up:

(3+2) + (4+2) + (5+2) + (6+2) = 5 + 6 + 7 + 8 = 26

So, here is the answer:

$$\sum_{k=3}^{6} k + 2 = 26$$

$$3)\ \sum_{j=0}^{2} j^3 =$$

Answer: In this problem, the variable is j. Start with a value for j of 0 and end with a value for j of 2, so the numbers you will use for j are 0, 1, and 2. Now plug these numbers, one at a time, into the operation j^3, and add them all up:

$0^3 + 1^3 + 2^3 = \quad 0 + 1 + 8 = \quad 9$

Here is the answer:

$$\sum_{j=0}^{2} j^3 = 9$$

lim

Lim stands for Limit, which is a key concept in calculus. Limits tell you what you are getting ***close to***, which is a different way of thinking than how we usually think of an answer. Limit problems ask this question:

"What **y value** do you get *closer and closer to* when x gets *closer and closer to* a certain number?"

The graph of $y = x^2$ on the next page shows visually what you are doing when you find a limit.

First, look at the x-axis and notice the arrows approaching 3 from either side. This shows the x values getting closer and closer to 3, both from the right side and from the left side.

As a result, the y values along the curve of $y = x^2$ get closer and closer to 9. Therefore, the limit equals 9!

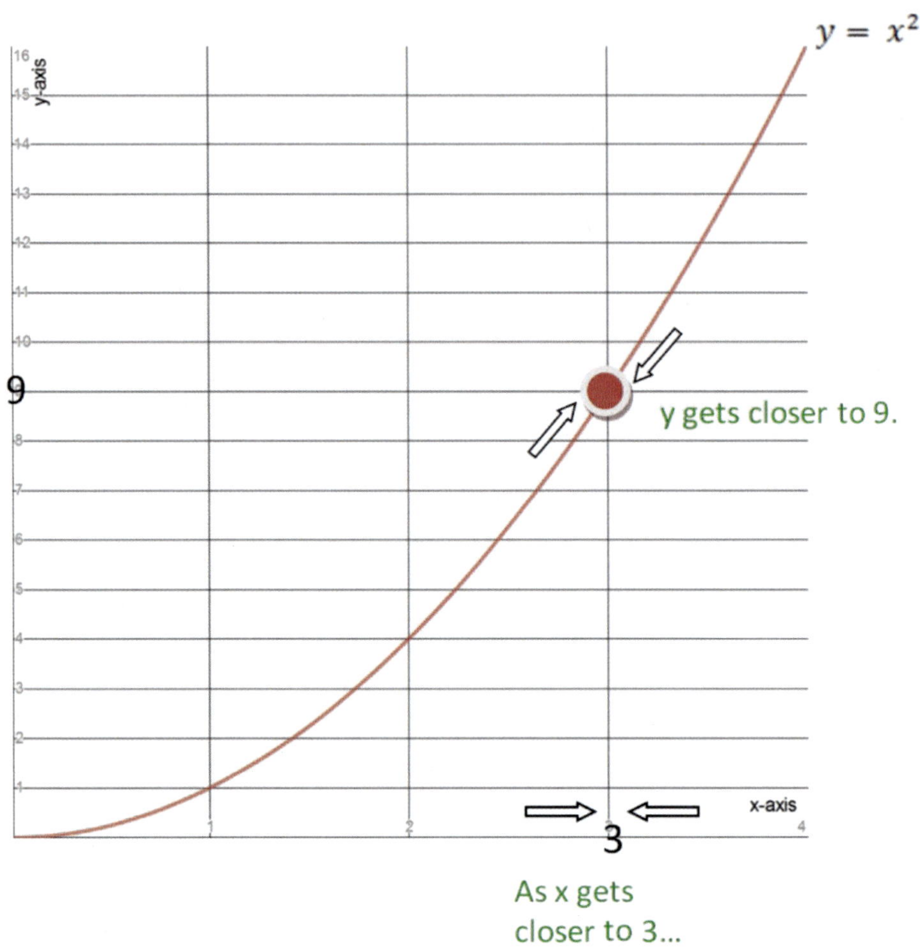

The limit equation for the above situation looks like this:

$$\lim_{x \to 3} x^2 = 9$$

and you would read it like this: "The limit as x approaches three of x squared equals 9."

There are three parts of the previous limit equation to pay attention to:

1) Under the word lim, there is a small x with an arrow and then the number 3 (this could be any number, but in this example it is 3). This tells you that you are going to make your x values get closer and closer to 3.

$$\lim_{x \to 3} x^2 = 9$$

2) To the right of the word lim is an operation, in this case x^2 (this comes from the curve equation $y = x^2$).

$$\lim_{x \to 3} x^2 = 9$$

3) After the equal sign is the y value you "approach." By plugging x values ***closer and closer to*** 3 into x^2, you get y values ***closer and closer to*** 9.

$$\lim_{x \to 3} x^2 = 9$$

In this problem, you could have gotten the answer by simply plugging the x value of 3 into x^2 and getting the value of 9. In this case, y didn't just come close to 9, y actually equaled 9. But limits don't care what y equals! The answer to a limit problem is what number y gets *close to*, not what it equals.

The idea of limits becomes more interesting when you can't just plug in the x value to get the answer.

Here is an example:

$$\lim_{x \to 2} \frac{x^2 - 4}{x - 2} =$$

In this problem, x is approaching 2. But, if you try to plug in 2 for x in the operation, you get zero in the denominator, which is not allowed! The graph on the next page shows what is happening.

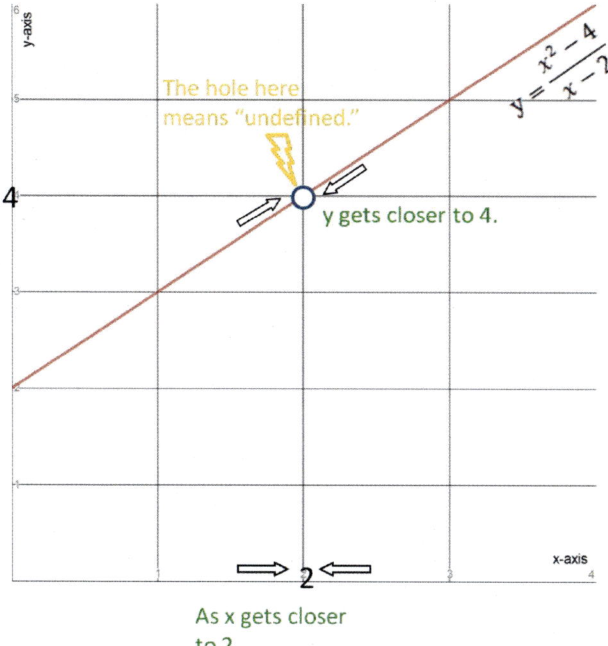

Notice the "hole" when x = 2 because the function is "undefined" here (it has zero in the denominator when x = 2). That means there is absolutely never a y value when x = 2. This is where limits come in handy because they enable you to get an answer anyway!

You just need to look at what y value you get ***closer and closer to*** as x gets ***closer and closer to*** 2. From the graph above, you can see that as x approaches 2, the y value approaches 4. So, the answer to this limit problem is 4.

$$\lim_{x \to 2} \frac{x^2 - 4}{x - 2} = 4$$

In this case, even though you couldn't find an answer to "What does y equal when $x = 2$," you ***could*** still find the answer to "What does y come really, really ***close to*** when x comes really, really ***close to*** 2."

Sometimes in limit problems, x doesn't approach a number; instead, it approaches infinity. Look at the graph below of $y = x^3$.

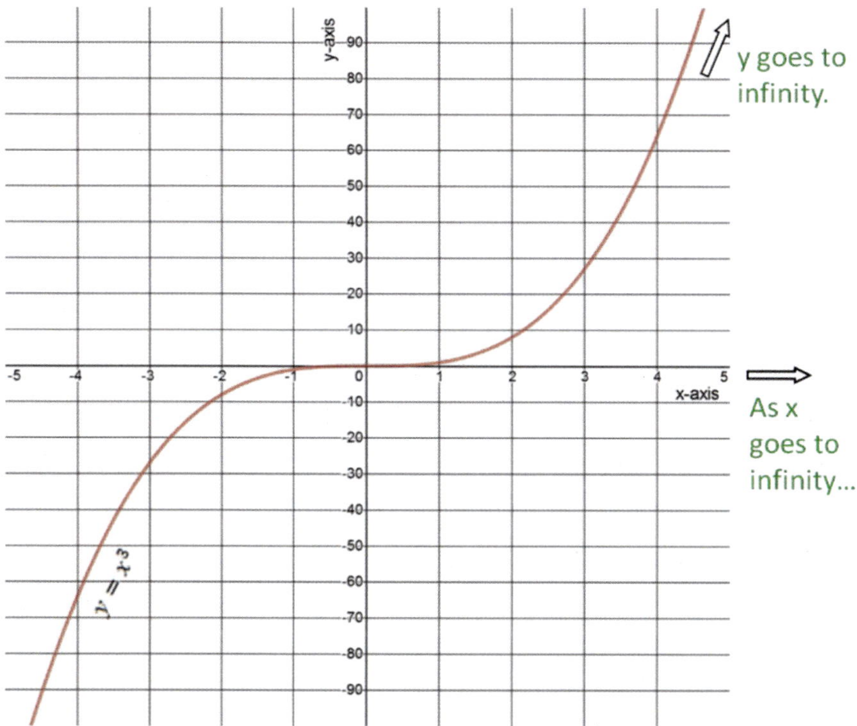

From the graph, you can see that as x values get larger, y values increase higher and higher, going up forever. So, as x values get ***closer and closer to*** infinity, y values get ***closer and closer to*** … infinity! Remember: the answer to limit problems is the y value you "approach." So, the answer to this limit problem is ∞ because that is what y is approaching.

Here is the answer in words and in an equation:

The limit as x approaches infinity of x^3 equals infinity:

$$\lim_{x \to \infty} x^3 = \infty$$

You could have gotten the same answer by plugging in the x value of ∞ into the operation x^3 to get ∞^3. Since there is nothing bigger than infinity, the answer is that y simply approaches infinity.

PROBLEMS

1) $\lim_{x \to \infty} x + 3 =$

Answer: Look at the graph below of $y = x + 3$. You can see that as x approaches infinity, y also goes to infinity.

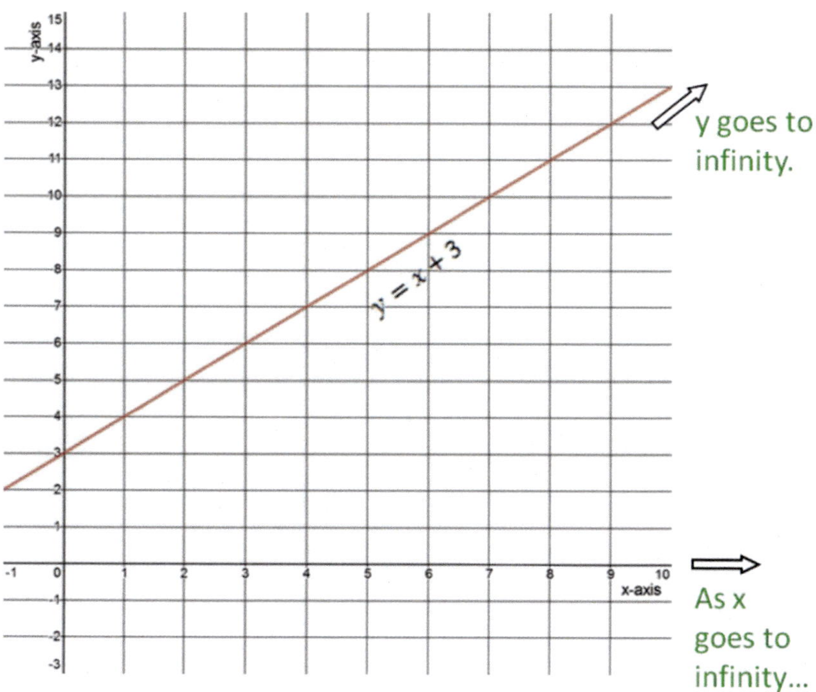

You can also get the answer by just plugging in ∞ for x in the operation $x + 3$. This would give you ∞ + 3, which is still just ∞ (you can't get any higher than ∞)! Either way, the answer is

$$\lim_{x \to \infty} x + 3 = \infty$$

2) $\lim_{x \to 9} \frac{x}{9} =$

Answer: Since x is approaching 9 in this problem, try plugging in the x value of 9 into the operation $\frac{x}{9}$. This works (you don't get zero in the denominator)!

Plugging in 9 produces $\frac{9}{9}$ or 1.

You can also see from the graph on the next page that as x values approach 9 from either side, the y values get closer and closer to 1. In this case, y actually reaches 1, but it doesn't matter in limit problems; the answer is the same whether or not y actually gets to the number.

$$\lim_{x \to 9} \frac{x}{9} = 1$$

Here is the graph showing what is happening in this problem:

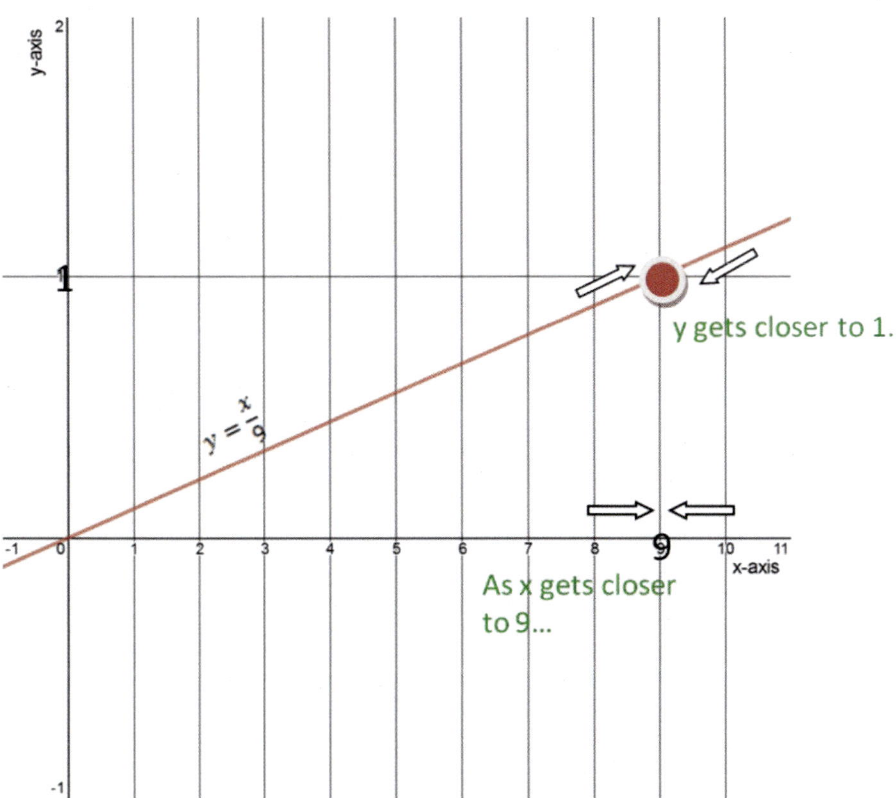

3) Using the graph below, solve the following limit problem:

$$\lim_{x \to \infty} \frac{x-2}{x} =$$

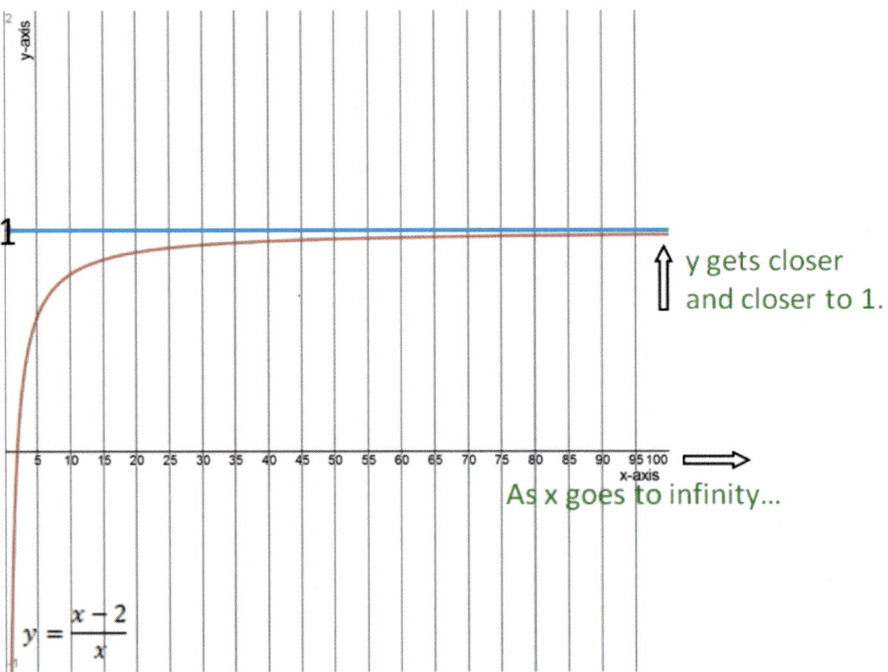

You can see that as x gets bigger and bigger, the y values are getting closer and closer to 1. Look at what the y value is when x is 100 (the last number included on the x-axis on our graph) – it is really, really close to 1! In fact, the larger the x values get, the closer to 1 the y values will get.

Interestingly, y will never, ever actually reach 1. But, we can still answer the question of what number y gets really, really ***close to*** as x approaches infinity. That number is 1, and that is the answer to the limit problem:

$$\lim_{x \to \infty} \frac{x-2}{x} = 1$$

Note: As mentioned previously, an asymptote is a line that a curve comes ever-closer to but never reaches. In this problem, the blue horizontal line where y equals 1 is an asymptote.

CALCULUS

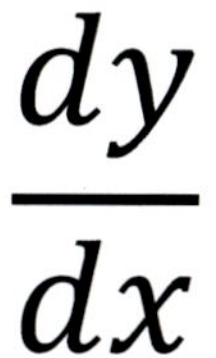

$$\frac{dy}{dx}$$

$$\frac{d}{dx}$$

$$y'$$

$$f'(x)$$

Derivatives are a big deal in calculus. There are different ways to write derivatives, but the most common ways are

$$\frac{dy}{dx} \qquad \frac{d}{dx} \qquad y' \qquad f'(x)$$

You can think of a derivative as a rate, rate of change, slope, or steepness.

You might already know how to find the rate of change, or slope, of a straight line from your math classes in middle school. But if not, here is a quick explanation of how to find the slope of the straight line shown below.

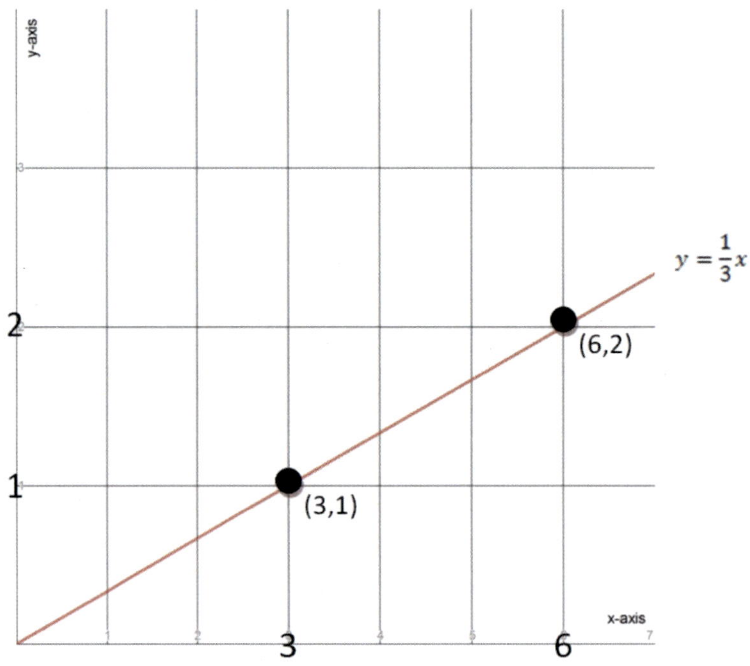

First, find two points on the line; in this case you can use the points (6, 2) and (3, 1). Then calculate the following, which are all different ways of saying the same thing:

$$\frac{the\ change\ in\ y}{the\ change\ in\ x}, \text{ or } \frac{\Delta y}{\Delta x}, \text{ or } \frac{the\ diference\ between\ y\ values}{the\ difference\ between\ x\ values}, \text{ or } \frac{rise}{run}$$

(The triangle in the fraction $\frac{\Delta y}{\Delta x}$ is called "delta" and means "change in").

In this problem, you have $\frac{2-1}{6-3}$, or $\frac{1}{3}$. So, the slope of this straight line is $\frac{1}{3}$.

On a straight line, the slope is the same all along the line. No matter what point you are on, the slope never changes.

Finding the slope of a curved line is harder because it keeps changing. The slope at one point on a curve is different from the slope at other points along the same curve (even if the points are infinitesimally close to each other).

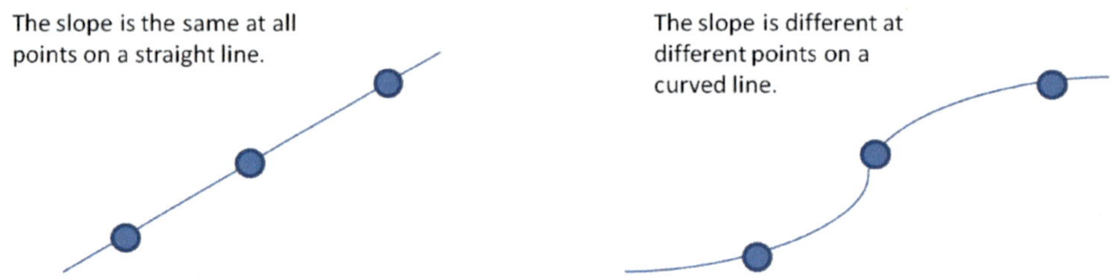

That is why derivatives are so useful – they enable you to find the slope at any particular point on a curved line.

Let's start with the curve $y = x^2$ shown below. Notice how the steepness of the curve is different at different points on the curve. Taking the derivative will enable us to find the slope anywhere along the curve.

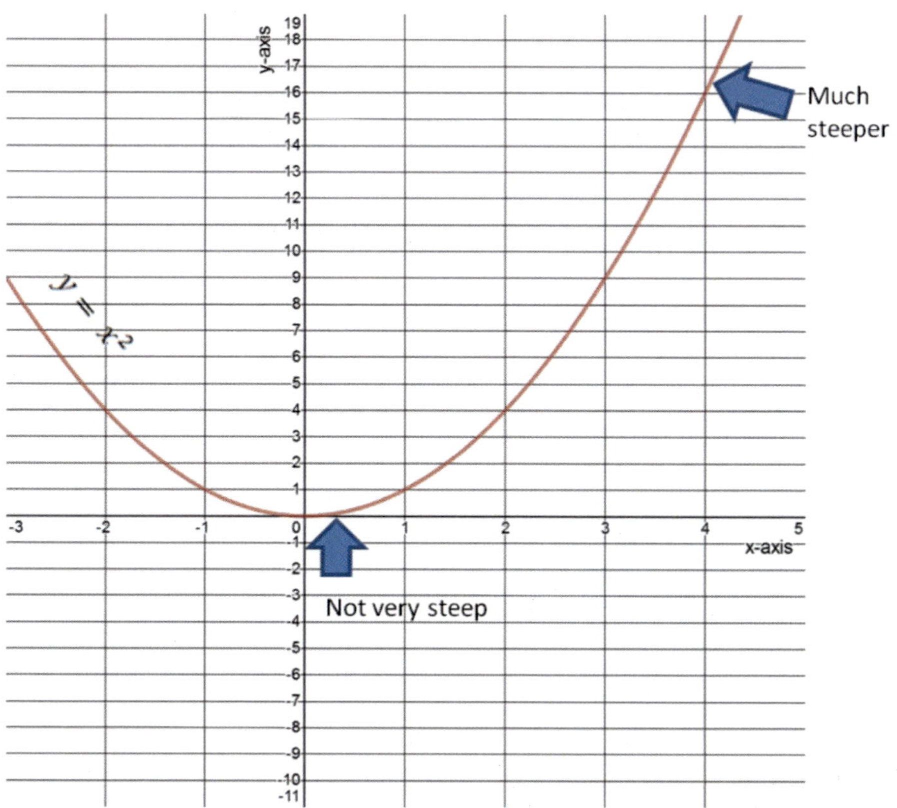

The first step is to write the derivative problem. Using the curve $y = x^2$ from our graph, just take the x^2 from the equation and put the derivative symbol in front of it:

$$\frac{dy}{dx}\,[x^2] =$$

There are lots and lots of rules for taking derivatives that you will learn later. For now, you can just learn this one very useful one called the Power Rule. You use it when you are taking the derivative of x to an exponent. It will work in our example here because x is being raised to an exponent.

The Power Rule has two steps:

1) put the exponent number in front of x,

$$X^{2}$$

2) reduce the exponent by 1.

$$X^{2 - 1}$$

In this example, you would put the exponent number 2 in front of x, then reduce the exponent by 1:

$2x^{(2-1)}$

Since $2x^{(2-1)}$ equals $2x^1$, and since that is the same as just $2x$, here is the answer:

$\frac{dy}{dx}\,[x^2] = 2x$

What you have found ($2x$) is the formula for finding the slope at ***ANY*** point along the curve that you are interested in.

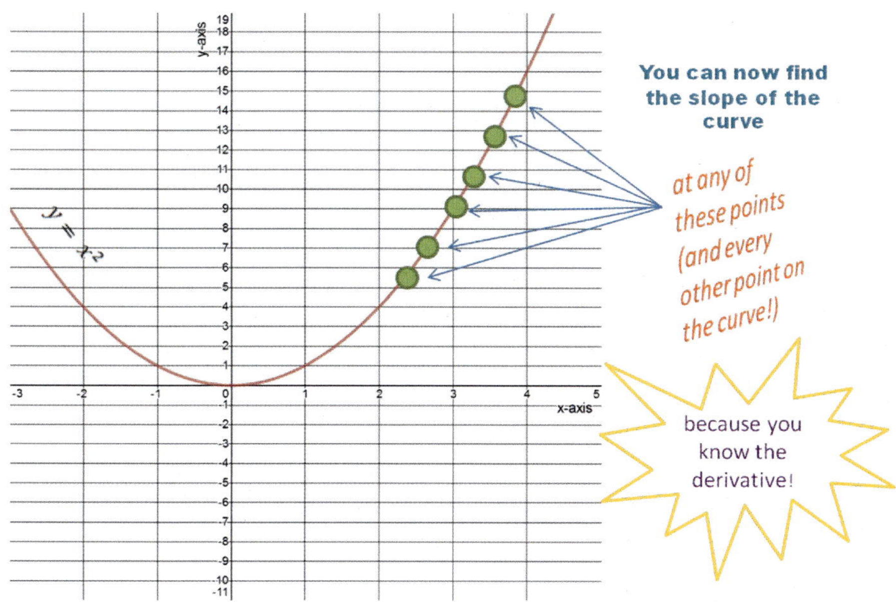

Let's see how this is done. We will choose the point (3, 9). All we need is the x-coordinate of this point (which is 3). Just plug 3 into the derivative formula you just found (which is $2x$), like this:

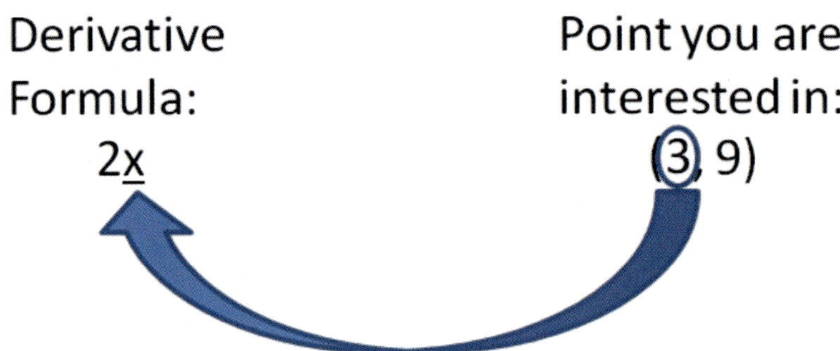

When you do that, you get 2*(3) = 6. You have now found the slope at a particular point on this curve. At the exact point (3, 9), the slope of the $y = x^2$ curve is 6.

If you had picked a different point, you would have plugged in its x-coordinate into the derivative formula $2x$, and you would have gotten a different answer for the slope. That is how you find the slope at any and all the different points on a curve: just plug in the x-coordinate of the point into the derivative formula.

What the derivative calculation is ***actually*** doing is giving you the slope of what is called the **Tangent Line**. Tangent Lines are a key concept of derivatives. A Tangent Line is a straight line that touches the curve at just one point.

There is a unique Tangent Line for every point on a curve. The slope of each Tangent Line tells you the slope of the curve at that particular point.

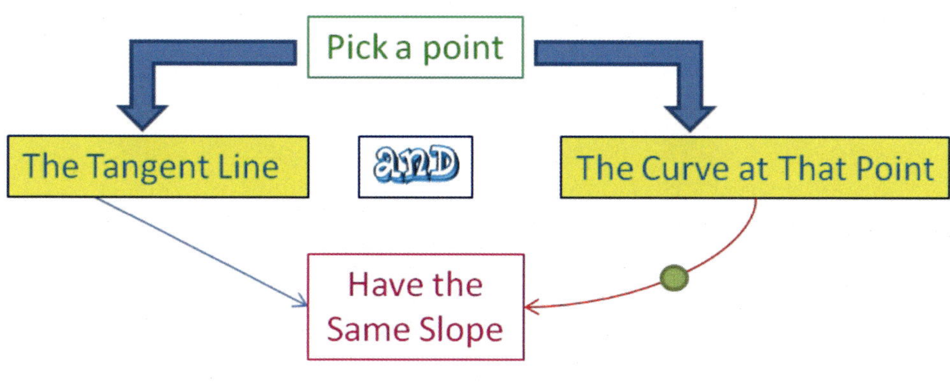

The graph below shows the Tangent Line from our example that touches the $y = x^2$ curve at the exact point (3, 9).

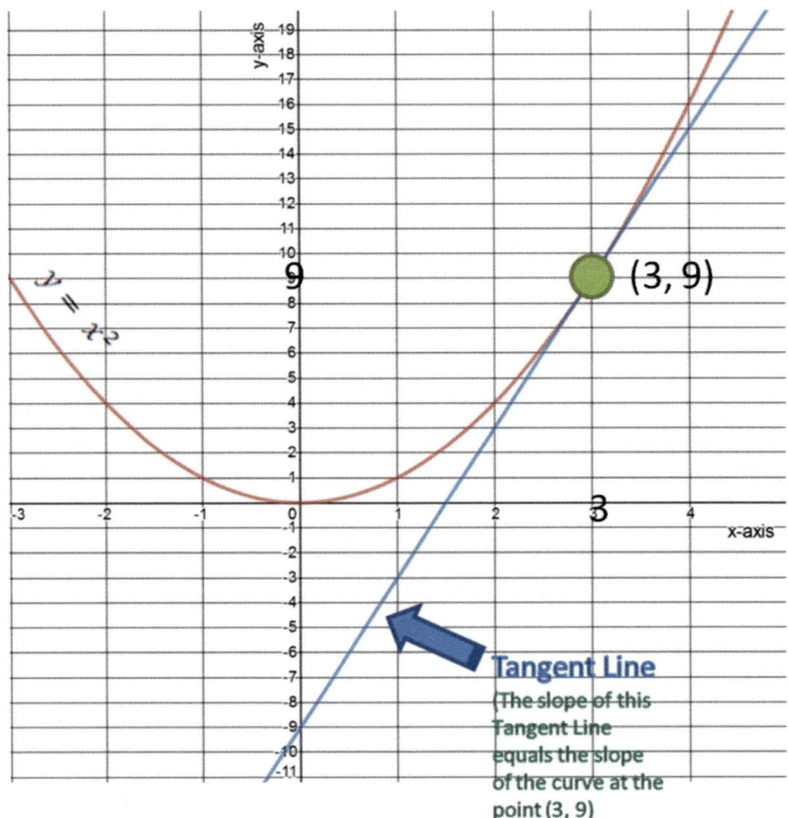

Note: Even though it looks like it touches more of the curve, the Tangent Line is only just really close to the curve near the point (3, 9) and only actually touches it right at that exact point.

You can see from this graph that the Tangent Line does indeed have a slope of 6, the answer that we got from our derivative calculation.

To prove this, calculate the $\frac{rise}{run}$ between the points (2, 3) and (3, 9) on the blue Tangent Line:

$$\frac{rise}{run} = \frac{9-3}{3-2} = \frac{6}{1} = 6$$

Both the slope of the Tangent Line and the slope of the curve at the point (3, 9) are the same: 6

One very useful way to use derivatives is for finding the exact minimum or maximum of a curve. A curve reaches its lowest point at the bottom of a "trough," and it reaches its highest point at the top of a "hill." At each of these points, the Tangent Line would be a horizontal line, as shown in the picture below, and the slope of any horizontal line is zero.

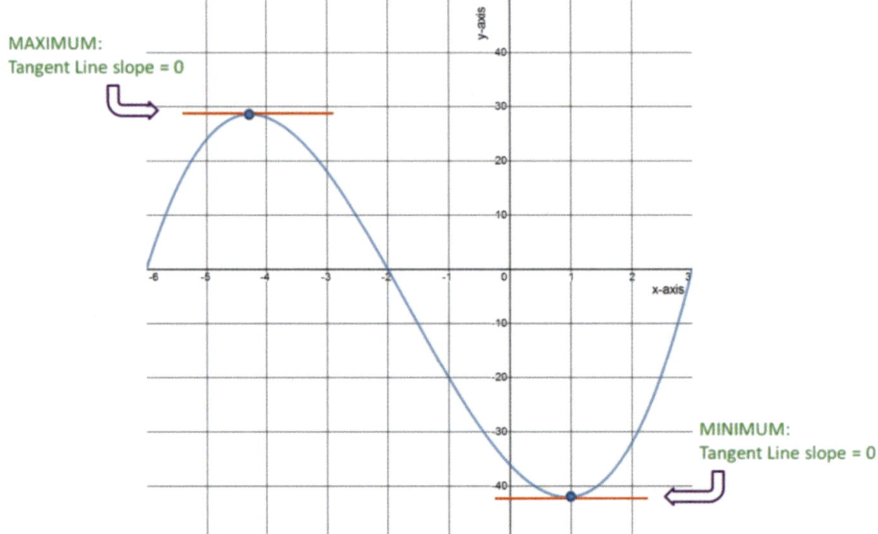

So, one way to find the maximum and minimum points of a curve is to find the derivative, and then set that derivative formula equal to zero. This works because the derivative is the slope of the Tangent Line, and you want to find where that slope equals zero. Let's see how this works in an example problem.

Problem: Find the minimum of the curve $y = x^2$

Answer: First, you would find the derivative, which we have already found previously in this chapter:

$$\frac{dy}{dx}[x^2] = 2x$$

Next, you would set that derivative formula to zero, because we want to find where the slope of the Tangent Line (the derivative) is zero.

$$2x = 0$$

Now, using algebra, divide by 2 on both sides of the equal sign, to get

$$x = 0$$

That means that the maximum or minimum point on your curve is the point that has an x-coordinate of 0. To find the y-coordinate of this point, plug 0 in for x into your original equation $y = x^2$. When you do that, you will get $y = 0^2$, or $y = 0$. So, at the point where the x-coordinate equals zero and the y-coordinate equals zero, which is the point (0, 0), we will have either a maximum or minimum.

If you look at the graph of $y = x^2$ again (shown below), you will see that the point (0, 0) occurs at the bottom of a "trough." Therefore, the point (0, 0) is the minimum point of the $y = x^2$ curve.

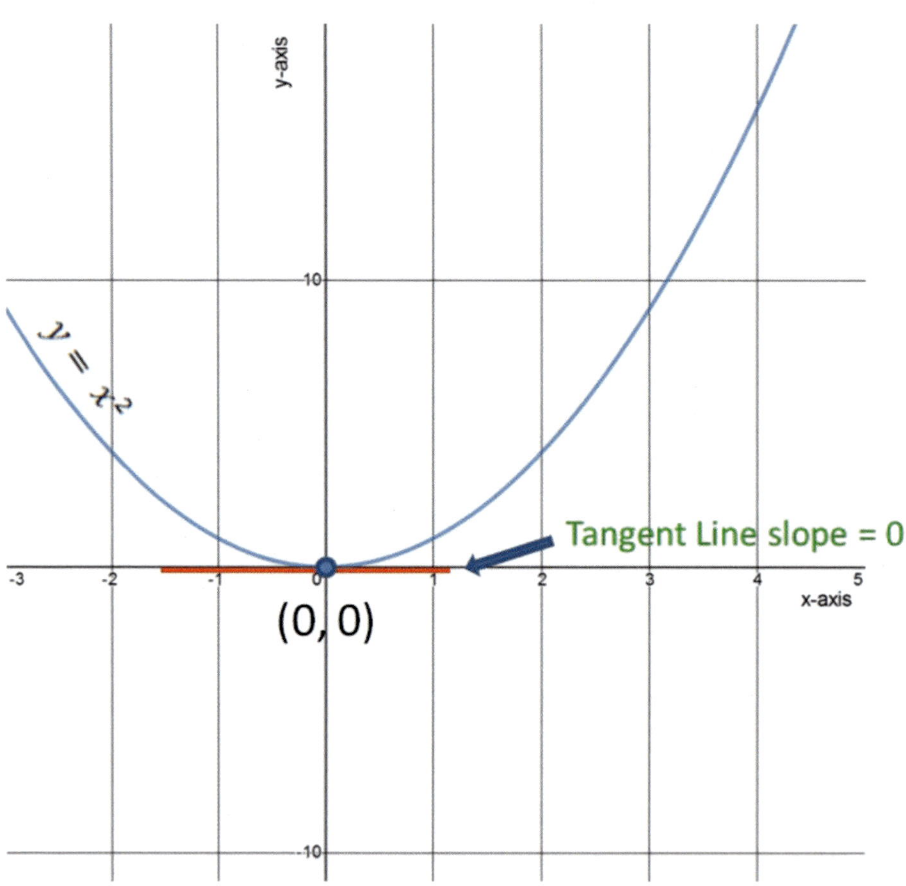

PROBLEMS

1) $\frac{dy}{dx}\,[x^3] =$

Answer: Use the Power Rule to find the answer by putting the exponent number in front of x, then subtracting 1 from the exponent: $3x^{(3-1)}$. The answer, which gives you the formula for finding the slope of the $y = x^3$ curve anywhere along the curve, is

$$\frac{dy}{dx}\,[x^3] = 3x^2$$

2) Now, find the slope of the $y = x^3$ curve at the point (1, 1).

Answer: Plug in the x-coordinate of the point (which is 1) into the answer from problem 1 above (which is $3x^2$). That gives you $3(1)^2$ = 3. The answer is

The slope of the $y = x^3$ curve at the point (1, 1) equals 3.

Note: The graph below shows you visually what you did in this problem. When you found the derivative of x^3 at the point (1, 1), you found the slope of the Tangent Line to the curve at that particular point.

The straight blue line is that Tangent Line, and you can see on the graph that it does indeed have a slope of 3. To prove this, calculate the $\frac{rise}{run}$ between these points on the Tangent Line: (0, -2) and (1, 1)

$$\frac{rise}{run} = \frac{1--2}{1-0} = \frac{1+2}{1-0} = \frac{3}{1} = 3$$

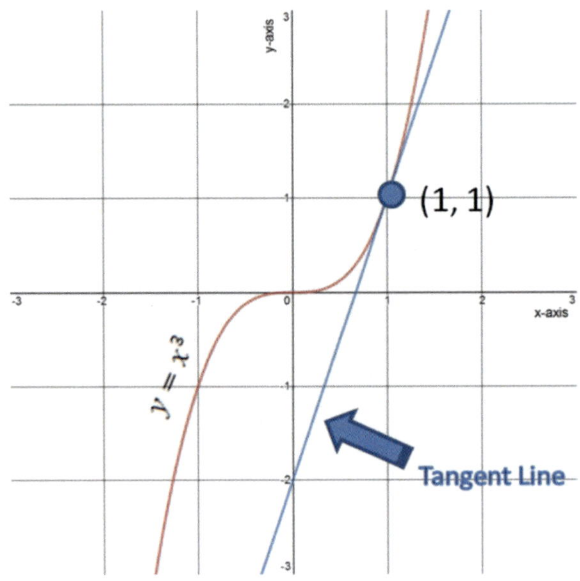

3) $\frac{dy}{dx}\,[x^4 + 3] =$

Answer: This derivative problem has two terms in it, something we haven't seen yet. When you are taking the derivative of more than one term, all you have to do is take the derivative of each term and add the results together, like this:

$\frac{dy}{dx}\,[x^4] + \frac{dy}{dx}\,[3] =$

Use the Power Rule to find the answer to the first piece: put the exponent number in front of x, then subtracting 1 from the exponent: $4x^{(4-1)}$ or $4x^3$.

For the second piece, you need to know this rule: the derivative of a constant (a plain number without a variable) is zero.

$$\frac{dy}{dx}\,[x^4 + 3] = 4x^3$$

4) $\frac{dy}{dx}\ [2x^5] =$

Answer: Use the Power Rule like in the previous examples, but in this case, there is already a number in front of x. So you need to multiply 2 (the existing number in front of x) by 5 (the exponent number that you need to put in front of x). Then, you subtract 1 from the exponent: $(2 * 5)x^{(5-1)}$. The answer is

$$\frac{dy}{dx}\ [2x^5] = 10x^4$$

5) $\frac{dy}{dx}\ [7x^3] =$

Answer: Use the Power Rule like in the previous examples, but again, there is already a number in front of x. So you need to multiply 7 (the existing number in front of x) by 3 (the exponent number that you need to put in front of x). Then, you subtract 1 from the exponent: $(7 * 3)x^{(3-1)}$.

$$\frac{dy}{dx}\ [7x^3] = 21x^2$$

6) Now, find the slope of the $y = 7x^3$ curve at the point (-1, -7).

Answer: Plug in the x-coordinate of the point (which is -1) into the answer from problem five (which is $21x^2$). That gives you $21(-1)^2$ = 21. So, here is the answer:

The slope of the $y = 7x^3$ curve at the point (-1, -7) equals 21

The graph below shows you visually what you did in this problem. When you found the derivative of $7x^3$ at the point (-1, -7), you found the slope of the Tangent Line. Its slope is the same as the slope of the curve at the point (-1, -7).

You can see that the slope of 21 is quite steep! On the Tangent Line, look at the two points (-1, -7) and (0, 14). You can see that the Tangent Line "rises" 21 units (from a y-coordinate of -7 to 14) as it "runs" 1 unit (from an x-coordinate of -1 to 0).

$$\frac{rise}{run} = \frac{21}{1} = 21$$

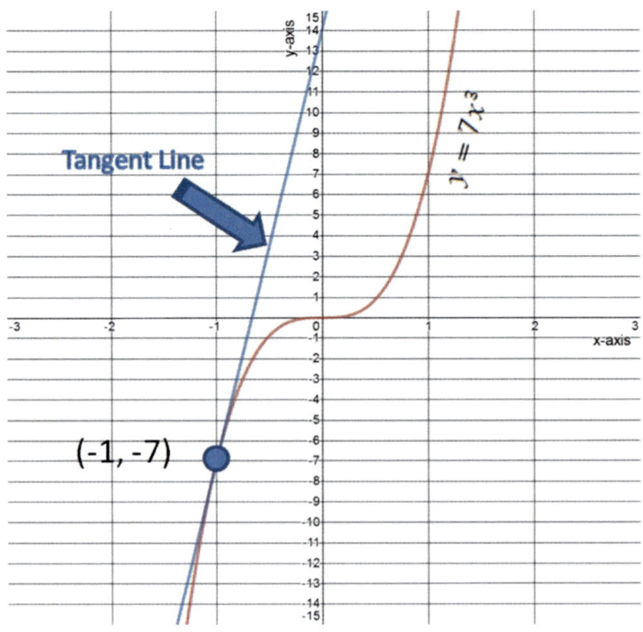

Along with derivatives, integrals are what calculus is all about! This symbol

$\int$

is the integral sign. Taking the integral, or integrating, means you are finding the area under the curve of a graph. Let's take a look at this integral:

$$\int_1^2 3x^2 \; dx =$$

There are five parts of the integral equation above to pay attention to:

1) The little number at the bottom of the symbol tells you what x value to start with.

$$\int_{1}^2 3x^2 \; dx =$$

2) The little number at the top of the symbol tells you what x value to end with.

$$\int_1^{2} 3x^2 \; dx =$$

3) To the right of the symbol is an operation, in this case $3x^2$. The curve you draw will be the graph of the equation $y = 3x^2$ (to get the curve equation, you just need to add "$y =$" to the operation).

$$\int_1^2 3x^2 \, dx =$$

4) Next to the operation is the notation "dx." This notation is included in the integral problem, but you can ignore it most of the time and definitely for our purposes here. It basically just tells you that x is the variable you are working with. It disappears when you take away the $\int$ sign while you are solving.

$$\int_1^2 3x^2 \, dx =$$

5) The answer after the equal sign (which we don't have yet in this problem) tells you what the area is under the curve of $y = 3x^2$ between the x values of 1 and 2 on the x-axis.

$$\int_1^2 3x^2 \, dx = \textit{Area under the curve}$$

On the graph below, you can see these starting and ending x values along the x-axis (1 and 2) and also the curve $y = 3x^2$ (the red curve). Highlighted in blue is what you are trying to find: the area under the curve.

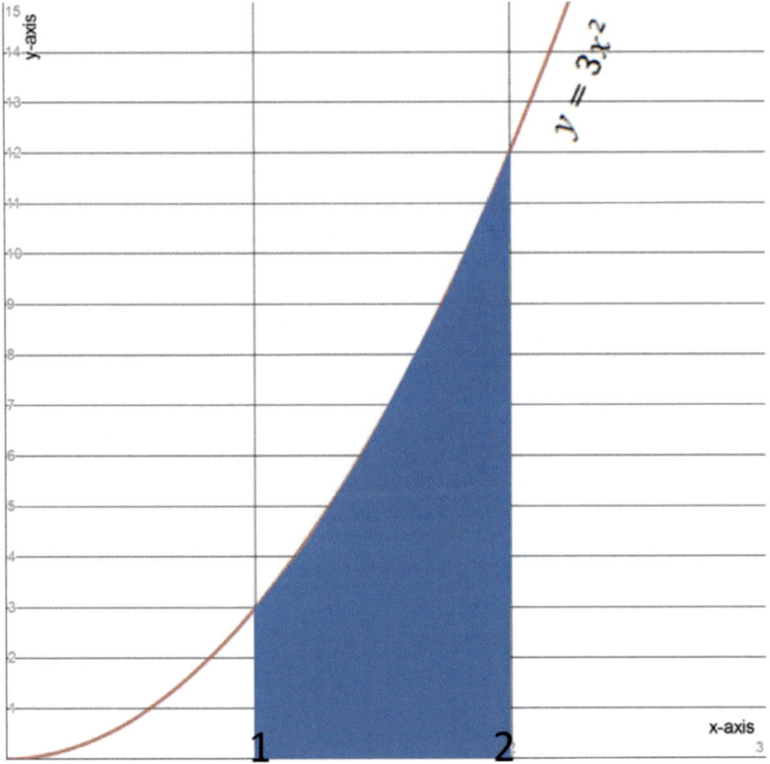

This is not a shape that we know an area formula for! That is where integrals come in handy. They provide a way for us to find the area of weirdly shaped figures.

Taking the integral is based on a pretty basic idea: let's just add up the areas of a bunch of rectangles that we could draw inside this blue space, as shown below.

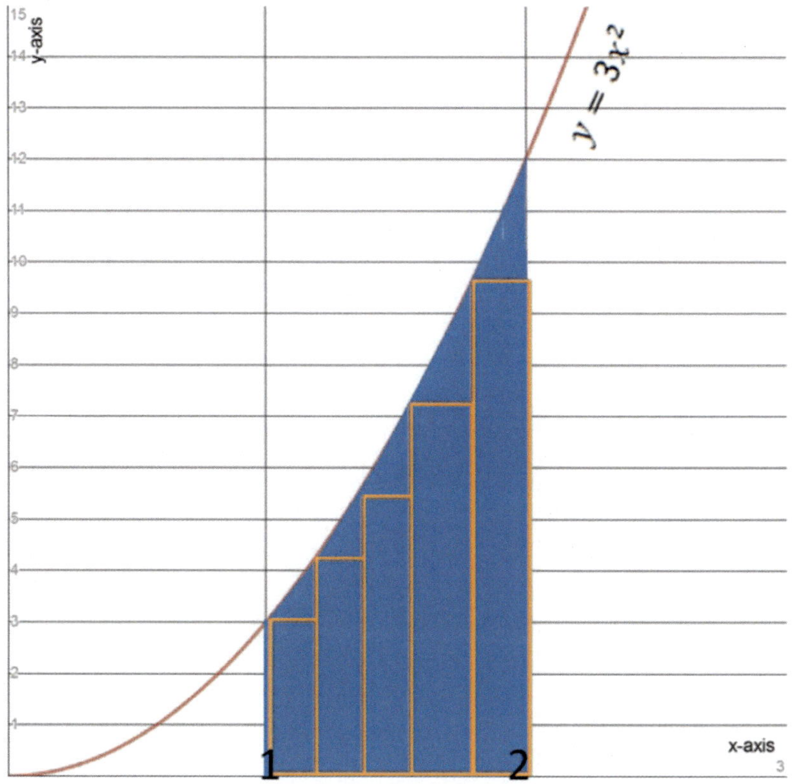

Here, I drew in five rectangles. Finding the areas of these rectangles would be pretty easy (just length times width), and I would add up their areas to get an estimate of the blue area under the curve. But, look at all that blue space that is outside of the rectangles. That space won't be counted if I just add up the areas of these five rectangles!

So, how about fitting more rectangles into that blue space by making the rectangles skinnier, like in the graph below?

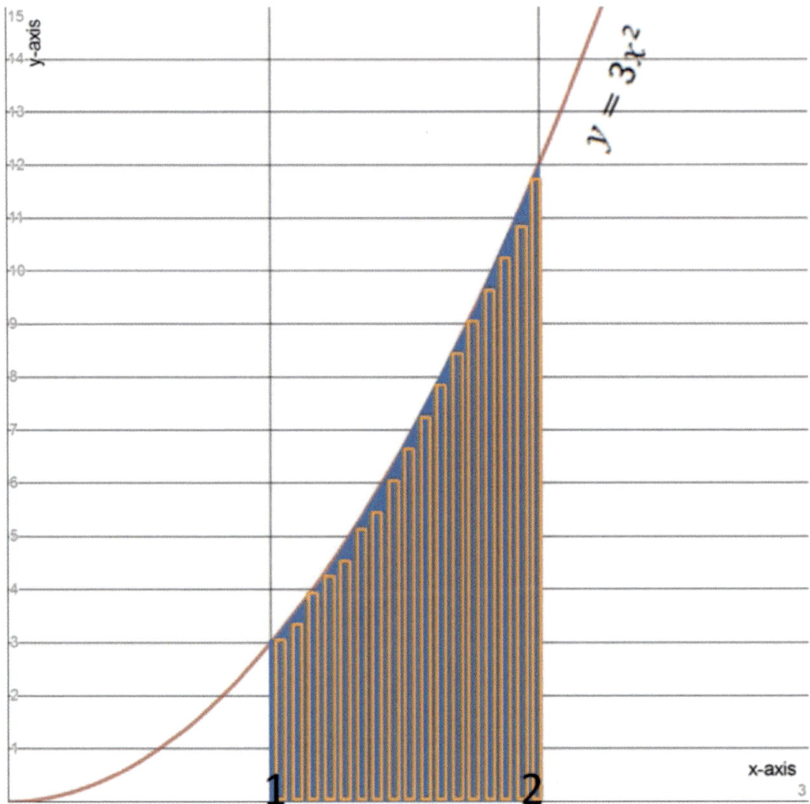

You can see that the skinnier you make the rectangles, the less blue space will be outside of the rectangles, and the more accurate your answer will be for "What is the area of the blue space?"

In fact, if you could make the rectangles infinitesimally skinny, you could fit an infinite number of rectangles into that blue space – that would give you a very accurate answer to your area question!

That is what taking the integral is basically doing: finding the area under a curve by adding up an infinite number of rectangles.

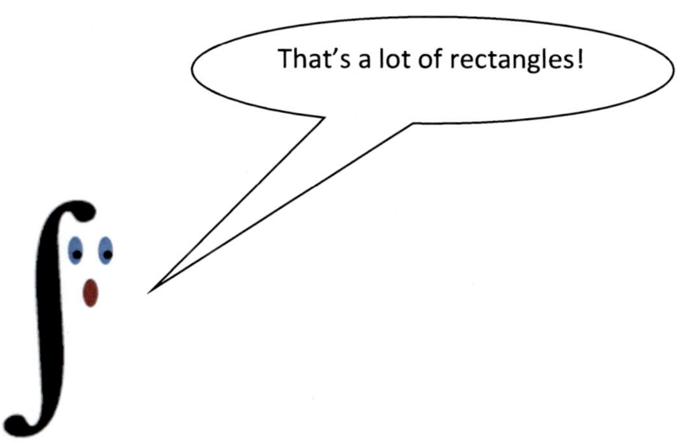

Before we get to how to solve an integral problem, there are two kinds of integrals to be aware of:

1) <u>Definite Integrals</u>: These have the little starting and ending x values on the bottom and top of the integral sign, like our example: $\int_1^2 3x^2 \ dx$

2) <u>Indefinite Integrals</u>: these do **NOT** have these little numbers, for example: $\int 3x^2 \ dx$

The same rules of integration apply to definite and indefinite integrals, but with definite integrals, you need to take a few more steps to solve for the particular given x values.

The answers for indefinite integrals, because they are not specific to particular x values, are left in a more general form. All you need to know about this more general form for now is that you add "+ C" to the answer for indefinite integrals.

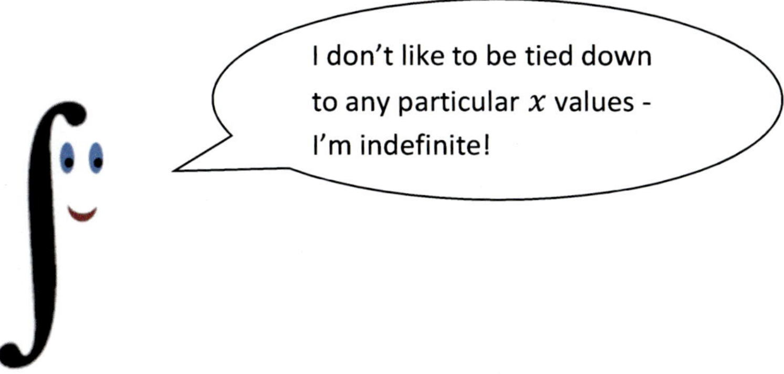

Just like we did with derivatives, let's learn one basic rule of integration that you can use to solve quite a lot of integral problems.

It is called the General Power Rule for Integration and you use it when you are taking the integral of x to an exponent.

Let’s use this rule on this indefinite integral:

$\int x^3 \ dx =$

The General Power Rule for Integration has two steps:

1) Add 1 to the exponent
2) Divide by the answer you got in step one

In this example, you would

1) Add 1 to the exponent of 3
2) Divide by that answer: 4

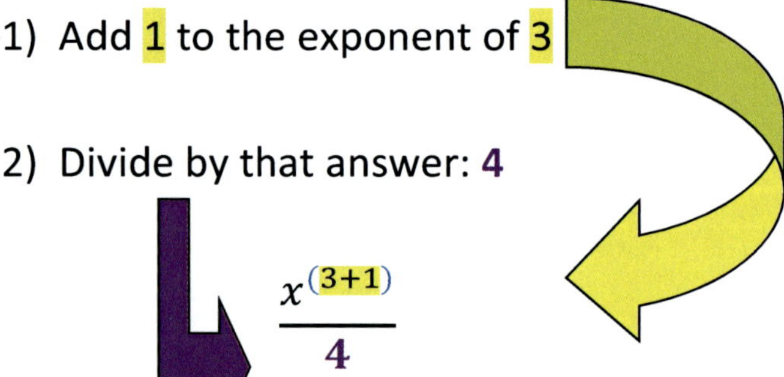

Since this is an indefinite integral, you need to add “+ C” to the answer. Here is the answer to the problem:

$\int x^3 \, dx = \frac{x^4}{4} + C$

That’s it if you are dealing with an indefinite integral!

Now, let's make that same problem a definite integral (by adding the little starting and ending x values on the bottom and top of the integral sign) and see what extra steps we do to solve it.

$$\int_0^5 x^3 \; dx =$$

Since the rules of integration are the same for definite and indefinite integrals, we can use the answer that we already found for the indefinite integral above: $\frac{x^4}{4}$ + C. But, we don't need the "+ C" because now we are dealing with a definite integral.

So, after the equal sign, write $\frac{x^4}{4}$. Then, we need to show that we are interested in just the x values starting at 0 and ending at 5. So, write these numbers after a square bracket like this:

$$\int_0^5 x^3 \; dx = \left.\frac{x^4}{4}\right]_0^5$$

What's next is the most amazing part and is so important that it is called the Fundamental Theorem of Calculus. With the simple calculation that follows, you will be able to find the answer to the question: "What is the area under the $y = x^3$ curve between the x values of 0 and 5?" No need to draw an infinite number of rectangles and add them all up! This is quite a shortcut! Here are the final steps starting from here:

$$\left.\frac{x^4}{4}\right]_0^5$$

- ✓ plug in 5 for x in $\frac{x^4}{4}$
- ✓ plug in 0 for x in $\frac{x^4}{4}$
- ✓ subtract the two answers

$$\frac{(5)^4}{4} - \frac{(0)^4}{4} = \qquad \frac{625}{4} - \frac{0}{4} = \qquad \frac{625}{4} = \qquad 156.25$$

Here is your final answer to the problem:

$$\int_0^5 x^3 \; dx = \left.\frac{x^4}{4}\right]_0^5 = 156.25 \text{ square units}$$

You found that the area under the $y = x^3$ curve between the x values of 0 and 5 along the x-axis is 156.25 square units. The picture below shows the blue area that you just found.

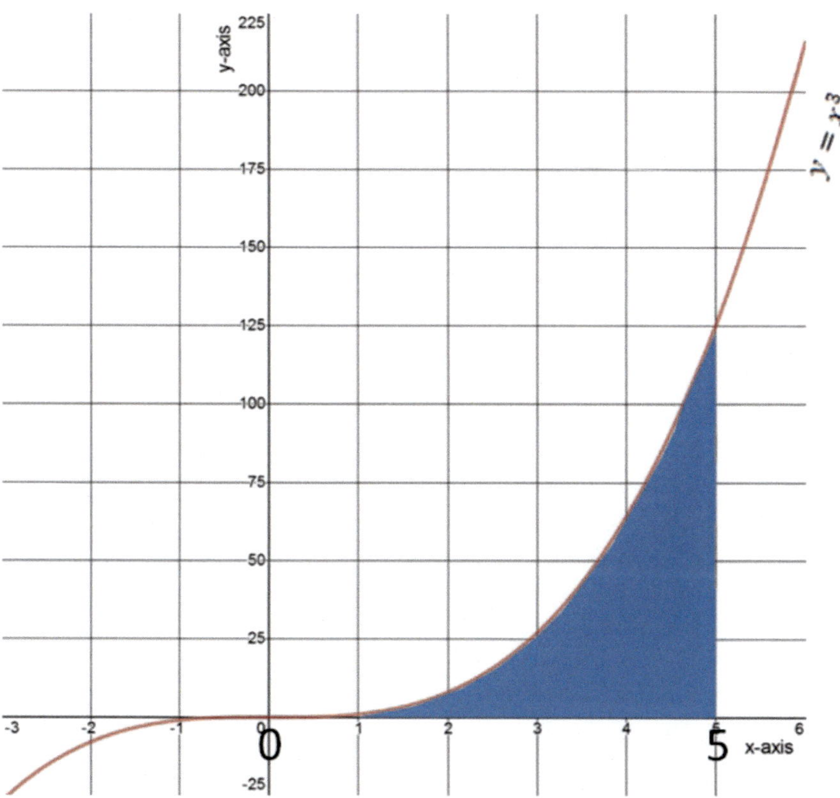

Amazing, right? You just found the area of a shape that doesn't have a simple area formula, like a square, rectangle, trapezoid, circle or triangle does. And it doesn't stop there! Using integrals, you can also find the volume of all sorts of interesting 3-dimensional shapes that don't have a nice formula like a cube, sphere, cylinder, or cone does.

Cool fact worth noting: derivatives and integrals are inverse operations, meaning they undo each other. In other words, if you take the derivative of something, then take the integral of that answer, you will get back to what you started with. Similarly, if you take the integral of something, then take the derivative of that answer, you will get back to what you started with.

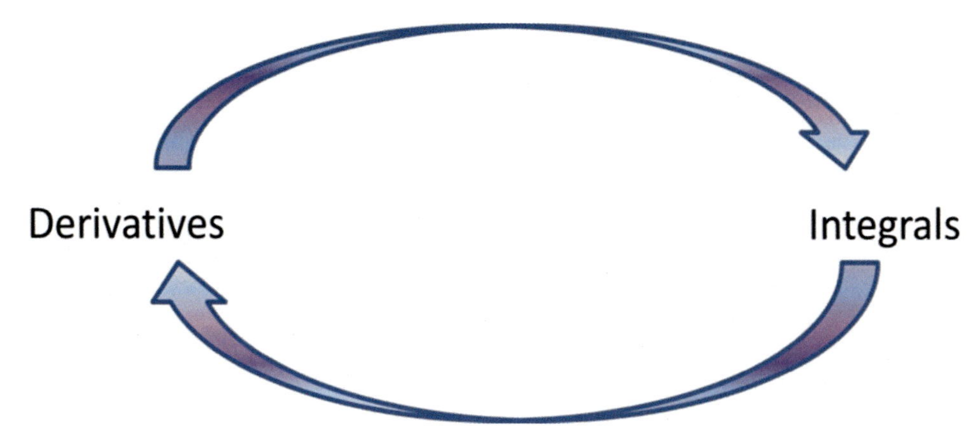

You can see this in the problem we just worked with:

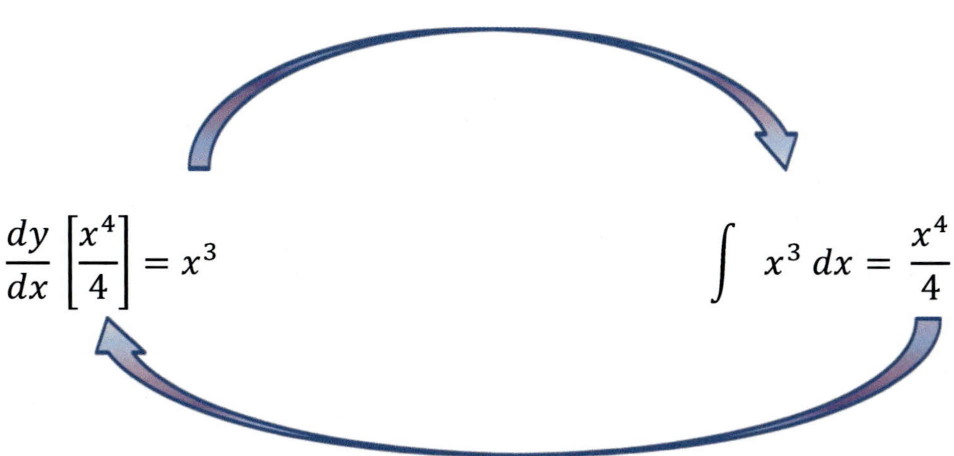

PROBLEMS

1) Estimate

$$\int_1^4 x^2\,dx =$$

by drawing 3 rectangles under the curve and adding up their areas.

Answer: Here is the graph of $y = x^2$ with 3 rectangles drawn in between the x values of 1 and 4:

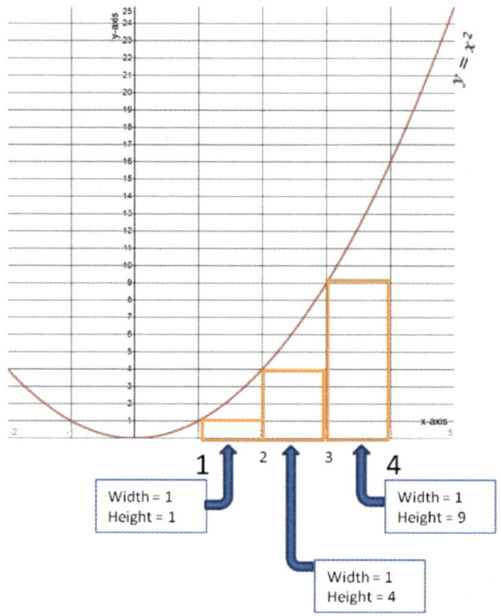

The areas of the rectangles are the width times the height of each one:

- First rectangle's area: 1*1 = 1
- Second rectangle's area: 1*4 = 4
- Third rectangle's area: 1*9 = 9

When you add the areas of the three rectangles up, you get 1 + 4 + 9 = 14. So, the answer is

The estimate of $\int_1^4 x^2 \, dx$ is 14 square units.

2) Now find the answer to $\int_1^4 x^2 \, dx$ by integrating.

Answer: Using the General Power Rule for Integration, you would add 1 to the exponent of 2 to get 3. Then, you would divide by that number 3:

$$\frac{x^{(2+1)}}{3} = \frac{x^3}{3}$$

Now, put the square bracket to the right of that answer with the little numbers on the bottom and top:

$$\int_1^4 x^2 \, dx = \left.\frac{x^3}{3}\right]_1^4$$

All you need to do now is plug in 4 for x, plug in 1 for x, and then subtract, like this:

$$\frac{(4)^3}{3} - \frac{(1)^3}{3} = \quad \frac{64}{3} - \frac{1}{3} = \quad \frac{63}{3} = \quad 21$$

Here is your final answer to the problem:

$$\int_1^4 x^2\,dx = \quad \left.\frac{x^3}{3}\right]_1^4 = \quad 21 \text{ square units}$$

Note: This is a bigger number than the answer to problem number 1 that estimated the answer by drawing the three rectangles. Notice in problem 1 how much space under the curve didn't get included in our rectangles! If we had used more rectangles, we would have gotten a more accurate answer. In fact, if we had used an infinite number of rectangles, we would have gotten the answer of 21 square units, which is the answer using integration.

3) $\int_2^9 x\ dx =$

Answer: The exponent on x in this problem is an understood 1. So, using the General Power Rule for Integration, you would add 1 to this exponent of 1 to get 2. Then, you would divide by that number 2:

$$\frac{x^{(1+1)}}{2} = \frac{x^2}{2}$$

Now, put the square bracket to the right of it with the little numbers on the bottom and the top:

$$\int_2^9 x\ dx = \frac{x^2}{2}\Bigg]_2^9$$

All you need to do now is plug in 9 for x, plug in 2 for x, and then subtract, like this:

$$\frac{(9)^2}{2} - \frac{(2)^2}{2} = \quad \frac{81}{2} - \frac{4}{2} = \quad \frac{77}{2} = \quad 38.5$$

$$\int_2^9 x\, dx = \frac{x^2}{2}\Bigg]_2^9 = 38.5 \text{ square units}$$

4) Using the graph below, find

$$\int_5^8 f(x)\, dx =$$

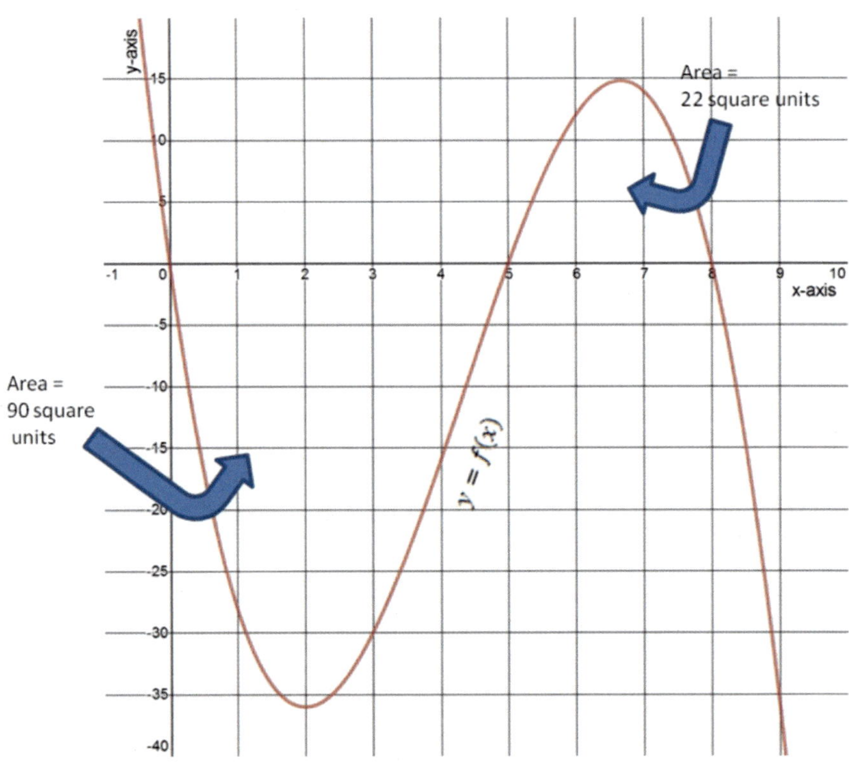

Answer: In this problem, the curve is just labeled $y = f(x)$, read y equals a function of x, which is just a simple way of naming the curve without showing the actual equation.

The problem gives the area calculations for the two enclosed spaces between the curve and the x-axis.

All you have to do is look at the little numbers at the bottom and the top of the integral sign in your problem to see what numbers on the x-axis you start and stop at. In this problem, you would start at 5 and end at 8 along the x-axis. The graph conveniently labels this area under the curve between the x values of 5 and 8. The answer is

$$\int_5^8 f(x)\ dx = 22 \text{ square units}$$

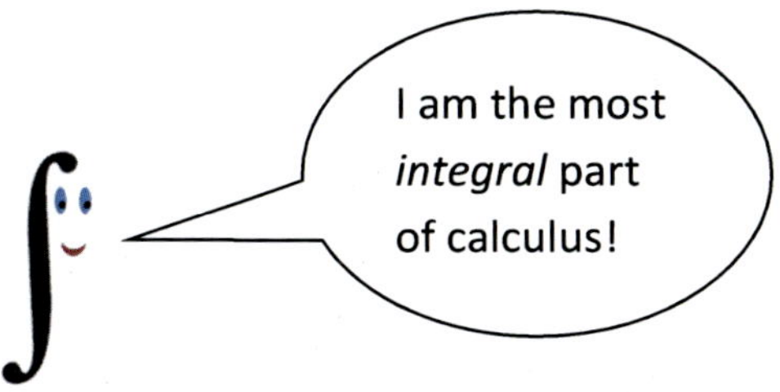

$$e^x$$

We are revisiting ***e*** because now that you know some calculus, you can appreciate a couple very cool features of this amazing number:

1) The derivative of e^x is e^x

2) The integral of e^x is e^x

Below is the graph of $y = e^x$. You can see what it means from the graph for the derivative of e^x to equal e^x and for the integral of e^x to equal e^x.

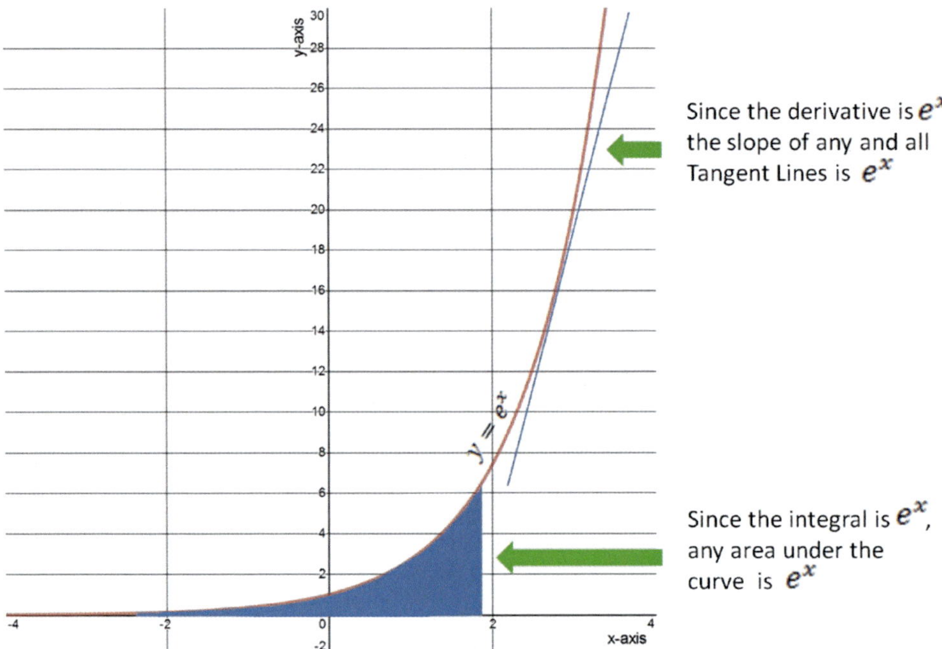

PROBLEMS

1) $\frac{dy}{dx}$ $[e^x] =$

Answer: The derivative of e^x is e^x:

$$\frac{dy}{dx} \; [e^x] = \; e^x$$

2) Find the slope of the $y = e^x$ curve at the point (1, 2.718)

Answer: Use the derivative formula you got as the answer to the first problem (which is e^x), then plug in the x-coordinate of your point (which is 1):

Plug 1 in for x into e^x
$e^1 = e$

The slope of the $y = e^x$ curve at the point (1, 2.718) equals e, or 2.718.

3) $\int e^x \, dx$ =

Answer: The integral of e^x is e^x. Since this is an indefinite integral, just remember to add "+ C":

$$\int e^x \, dx = e^x + C$$

4) $\int_0^1 e^x \, dx$ =

Answer: The integral of e^x is e^x. Now, put the square bracket to the right of that answer with the little numbers on the bottom and the top:

$$\int_0^1 e^x \, dx = e^x\Big]_0^1$$

Now plug in 1 for x, plug in 0 for x, and then subtract (remember: any number to an exponent of 0 equals 1)

$e^1 - e^0$ = e – 1= 2.718 – 1 = 1.718

$$\int_0^1 e^x \, dx = e^x\Big]_0^1 = 1.718 \text{ square units}$$

This answer tells you what the area is under the $y = e^x$ curve between the x values of 0 and 1. The graph below shows visually what you found.

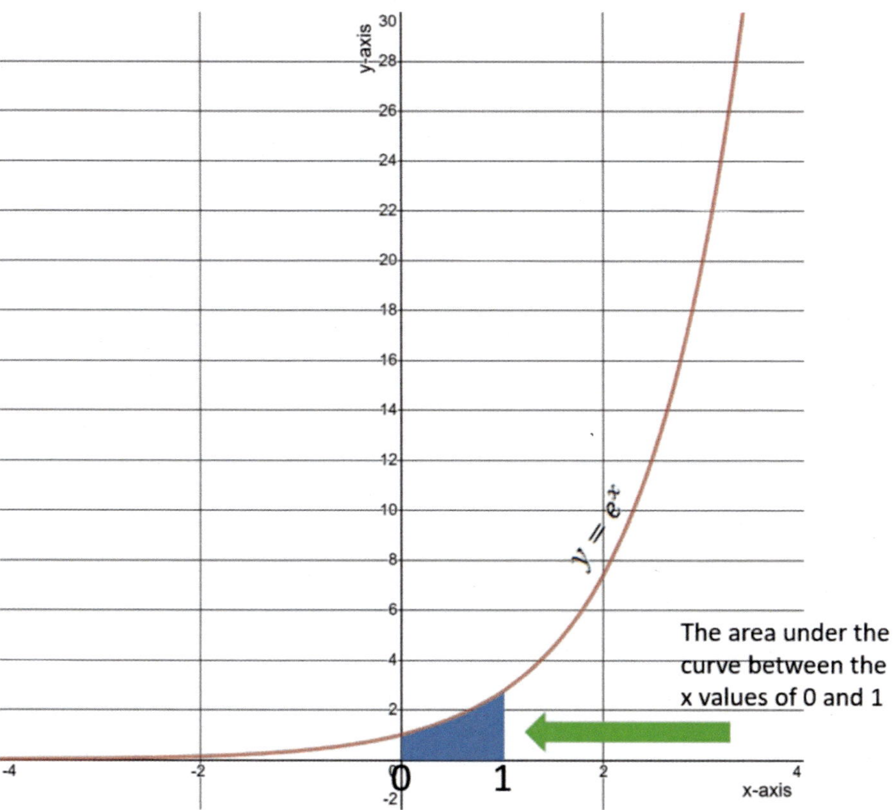

CONGRATULATIONS!

You now belong to the exclusive group of people who know how to do calculus! I hope that becoming familiar with these calculus symbols and rules will make calculus seem more comfortable and less daunting when you learn it in high school and college. Having a basic grasp of these important concepts should give you a great head start!

Acknowledgments

Thank you to my kids, Stephanie and Matthew, who helped me edit the book and who are the reason I decided to write it in the first place. Thank you to Paul, my husband, who encouraged me to do it. Thank you to my dad, Hugh, for all the great ideas, edits and suggestions.

About the Author

Serena Swegle is currently a high school tutor in the Seattle public school system and enjoys helping people get comfortable with math. She has previously worked as a CPA, financial analyst, public company stock researcher, investment banker and SEC staff member. She lives with her husband and two kids in Seattle, Washington and enjoys beach walks, tennis, badminton, and board games.

Made in the USA
Las Vegas, NV
25 November 2023